Dan Hultquist

Understanding

REVERSE

Answers to Common Questions—
Simplifying the New Reverse Mortgage

2017

For information, please contact:
Dan Hultquist
5828 Wembley Drive
Douglasville, GA 30135
email: dan@understandingreverse.com
website: www.understandingreverse.com

Cover design and book layout by Amy Hultquist, Visia, Inc.
Printed by CreateSpace, An Amazon.com Company

LEGAL DISCLAIMER
This book is presented solely for educational purposes. While best efforts have
been used in preparing this book, the author and publisher make no representations
or warranties of any kind and assume no liabilities of any kind with respect to
the accuracy or completeness of the contents and specifically disclaim any implied
warranties of merchantability or fitness of use for a particular purpose. Neither
the author nor the publisher shall be held liable or responsible to any person or entity
with respect to any loss or incidental or consequential damages caused, or alleged
to have been caused, directly or indirectly, by the information or programs contained
herein. Every lending institution and borrower scenario is unique, and the strategies
contained herein may not be suitable for your situation, and you should seek the
services of a competent professional before obtaining any financial services. The
names used in the examples are fictional. Any likeness to actual persons, either
living or dead, is strictly coincidental.

The examples and educational material contained in this book are not from HUD
or FHA and this document was not approved by HUD or any government agency.
Portions of federal regulations and guidelines have been highlighted in this book
for clarification. However, it is recommended that the relevant regulation be read
in full when needed.

"A reverse mortgage can be a useful tool in a personal financial plan for many retirees, but it is often overlooked. Much of that is due to misunderstanding. Dan Hultquist, a very knowledgeable reverse mortgage professional and trainer, understands the utility and mechanics of reverse mortgages and explains them well. This book is a much welcome addition to the literature on reverse mortgages."

Peter H. Bell, President and CEO
National Reverse Mortgage Lenders Association
Washington, DC

"With today's increasing need for proper financial planning for baby boomers and retirees, it is critical that the facts about reverse mortgages are explained in straight talk to all, including financial planners and trusted advisors. This book is an excellent resource for seniors and adult children who are looking for clear answers, definitions, and proper uses for reverse mortgages."

Jeffrey S. Taylor, Master CMB, President
Wendover Consulting, Inc.
Greensboro, NC

To my lovely and talented wife, Amy, who not

only understands "Reverse", but has agreed to once again

contribute to the design and layout of this edition.

I also would like to acknowledge the board, staff, and committee

members of the National Reverse Mortgage Lenders Association

(NRMLA).

NRMLA's Education Committee, has been committed to fulfilling

*the mission "**To create a better understanding of the reverse***

*****mortgage product by building quality educational resources*****

*****and making them available to industry members,*****

*****affiliates, and consumers.**"*

CONTENTS

INTRODUCTION

Top mortgage executives and finance professionals are encouraging their friends and family members to obtain Reverse Mortgages. In many cases, this is happening even when homeowners have no immediate need for them. As a result, I have been asked numerous times to speak to CPAs and Financial Planners, explaining why the affluent are now getting Reverse Mortgages.

Could there be significant non-traditional uses for Reverse Mortgages that create advantages for those who are financially sound? Could Reverse Mortgages help more than just those who are desperate and needy?

Yes, however the proper use for a Reverse Mortgage continues to be misunderstood by many, resulting in some using it for the wrong reasons. As the title of this book suggests, I feel there is a need to have a better understanding.

THE HOUSING CRISIS

The prevailing thought in the mortgage industry from 2000-2007 was that EVERYONE should own a home. The ability to repay was not a major concern because home values were rising. When the housing market slowed, however, the mortgage industry's faults were exposed.

During this time, I transitioned into housing counseling, where I was able to see the effects of sub-prime loans and non-traditional mortgage lending. At this point, any loan where balances have the ability to rise, often called "negative amortization loans," were frowned upon. They were blamed, in part, for the housing crisis, and many instinctively, and incorrectly, included Reverse Mortgages in this category.

I wondered why my clients couldn't leverage their home equity to pay their delinquent property charges. If they could, they could even pay for home upgrades, or even travel abroad. Of course, Reverse Mortgages allowed them to do this, and today many are living out their retirement years with no monthly principal and interest payment obligations.

I began to ask questions…many of the same questions you might have today. In fact, these are many of the same questions I received from brokers and loan originators on a daily basis as the Director of Training for a national Reverse Mortgage lender.

THE NEW REVERSE MORTGAGE

It wasn't until recently that many in the Reverse Mortgage industry and the financial planning community began to realize that this program was designed to do more than just solve an immediate financial crisis. The ability to obtain a Reverse Mortgage **early** in retirement, and then access liquid home equity **late** in retirement, was generally not discussed with prospective clients.

New regulations highlighted the benefits of a growing line of credit. These funds not only give retirees confidence that they will be less likely to run out of money, but they can also be used to take pressure off retirement portfolios, delay social security, manage retirees' adjusted gross incomes, and extend retirees' assets beyond what traditional retirement planning offers.

UNDERSTANDING REVERSE

For the last several years I have studied this loan program in search of the best ways to explain these concepts, and this serves as the basis for my writing. These explanations are clarified by using **EXAMPLES** and documentation of relevant **REFERENCES.**

So, along the way, we will look at illustrations that will appear as:

Let's look at an EXAMPLE

These are not to be considered quotes for specific loans, or even good faith estimates. These are demonstrations for educational purposes only.

I also tried my best to document where the Reverse Mortgage industry gets their guidance in answering these questions. This will appear in the form of:

Let's look at REFERENCES

This may include references to Handbooks from the U.S. Department of Housing and Urban Development (HUD), the Code of Federal Regulations, portions of the National Housing Act, the Federal Trade Commission, The National

(continued)

Reverse Mortgage Lenders Association (NRMLA), and the Federal Housing Administration (FHA) Mortgagee Letters that update the Handbook Policies. All of these serve as a way for our regulators to instruct lenders about what they can, and cannot, do.

Please note: A **Glossary of Key Terms** and a **Principal Limit Factors Quick Reference Guide** can be found at the back of this book.

The primary intent of this book is to educate a broad audience on the finer details of the Reverse Mortgage program. Whether you are a financial planner, a mortgage professional, counselor, Realtor, older homeowner, or other interested party, I believe this book will help you better understand Reverse Mortgages.

Although I no longer originate loans, I am a Certified Reverse Mortgage Professional (CRMP), and a member of the National Reverse Mortgage Lenders Association (NRMLA). My sincere hope is that you find this book helpful, and that the true power of this great program will be revealed to you.

Chapter 1

What is a REVERSE MORTGAGE?

In its most basic sense, a Reverse Mortgage is any loan secured by a home where repayment is deferred to a later date. Generally, a Reverse Mortgage is paid back when the home sells in the future. So, a Reverse Mortgage does not necessarily have to be structured as an FHA-insured Home Equity Conversion Mortgage (HECM), the popular product we will discuss in the this book.

In some cases, Reverse Mortgages are offered as a "Single-Purpose Reverse Mortgage" by a municipality or state, to address a homeowner's need to repair the home or pay property taxes. It can even be offered by a non-profit organization to address issues like medical care. A lien against the home is simply established, and the lender is generally repaid when the home sells at a later date.

There are also "Proprietary Reverse Mortgages" that lenders may offer that are not FHA-Insured. These are rare, but we expect to see more of these pop up in the coming years. For the remainder of our discussion, however, one can assume that "Reverse Mortgage" means the FHA-Insured loan product that comprises the overwhelming majority of Reverse Mortgages offered nationwide.

The word "REVERSE" is used for two primary reasons:

1. The flow of money generally moves in reverse.

Funds on traditional mortgages move FROM a borrower's bank account TO some large lender or servicer. Reverse mortgages, however, have the ability to move funds in a lump sum, or in monthly payments, FROM a lender or servicer back TO the borrower.

Flow of Money

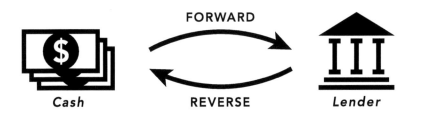

2. Loan balances tend to move in reverse.

Most traditional mortgages require principal and interest payments. This DECREASES the loan balance. Not requiring these payments may cause the loan balance to INCREASE instead.

Loan Balance

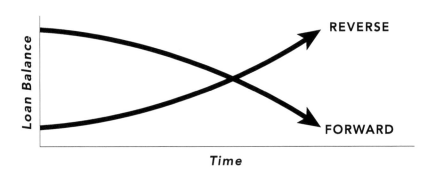

Since the flow of money generally moves in reverse, and the loan balances tend to move in reverse, it is obvious why this type of loan is called a Reverse Mortgage. However, a Reverse Mortgage doesn't have to operate in this way.

A DIFFERENT APPROACH

Many homeowners know that the Reverse Mortgage can convert a portion of home equity into cash for a specific immediate need. It is effective at assisting those that are "house rich, but cash poor," and it is used as a way of "cashing out" home equity during a financial crisis. It is clearly possible to stabilize a financial problem by accessing home equity with a Reverse Mortgage. It can even be used to purchase a home.

However, draws against home equity do not have to occur right away. In fact, they don't have to occur at all. There are financially savvy purposes for obtaining a Reverse Mortgage even if the homeowner isn't having a financial crisis. We will explore many reasons someone might obtain one outside of traditional usage of the product. For example, a homeowner at age 62 could establish a growing line of credit (LOC) that, depending on market conditions, could exceed even the home's value. This is not only a great way to have access to funds at any time, but it also may prove effective at assisting with financial planning. At any time, the homeowner could convert the growing line of credit into monthly payments for additional retirement income, pay for long-term care, or access funds from the line of credit if the retirement portfolio has been used up.

The need for this approach becomes clearer when we consider these statements:

- We don't know how long we are going to live.
- We don't know what financial pressures retirement will bring.
- We don't know how long our retirement funds will last.

There is a risk that older homeowners could run out of funds because of longevity, unforeseen financial pressures, or even poor performance of their retirement portfolio.

A Reverse Mortgage can be used in multiple ways. Using it to cash out a portion of the home's equity is one option. Using the purchase option to relocate to a new primary residence is another. And using it as a financial planning tool, as advocated by financial planners, leads to greater security and future cash flow options. As you will see, homeowners that convert their loan balances into a HECM, and establish a line of credit, are best equipped to diversify their home equity and manage home-ownership risks during retirement.

Let's look at REFERENCES

Federal Trade Commission: www.consumer.ftc.gov

If you're 62 or older—and looking for money to finance a home improvement, pay off your current mortgage, supplement your retirement income, or pay for healthcare expenses— you may be considering a reverse mortgage. It's a product that allows you to convert part of the equity in your home into cash without having to sell your home or pay additional monthly bills.

Chapter 2

What are the DIFFERENT USES
for Reverse Mortgages?

Since 2013, the federally-insured Reverse Mortgage program has gone through so many dramatic changes that it's no longer the Reverse Mortgage everyone thought it was. Some of the changes added consumer protections, while others radically altered the way Reverse Mortgages are obtained.

Unfortunately, many perfect candidates will continue to believe that a Reverse Mortgage is ONLY for a desperate homeowner with plenty of equity and no cash. I don't fault them for this—the most common Reverse Mortgage, the Home Equity Conversion Mortgage (HECM), has been marketed that way. However, recent modifications by the Federal Housing Administration (FHA) have highlighted the retirement planning advantages for the financially stable older homeowner. So, let me describe the three categories of homeowners who are now benefiting from a Reverse Mortgage.

Three Categories of Senior Homeowners

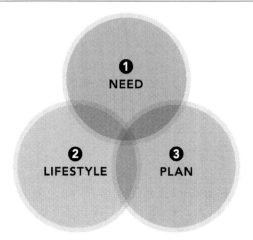

1. A Reverse Mortgage for immediate NEED

Generally, these traditional HECM borrowers are house rich and cash poor. And they need money now. In many cases, we can help them. A good example might be a homeowner who needs in-home care. Monthly payments generated by home equity conversion can help when they, or their heirs, are unable or unwilling to pay for these expenses.

Many people assume that the need for money is the ONLY reason to get a Reverse Mortgage. Yet, this traditional type of homeowner is a smaller piece of the pie now.

2. A Reverse Mortgage to enhance LIFESTYLE

Because a Reverse Mortgage does not require monthly principal and interest mortgage payments, obtaining one can help with cash flow. Yet, there are many other lifestyle advantages. Tenure payments are a form of monthly draw. Tenure means permanent, and these monthly payments will continue as long as the homeowner occupies the home. This is a great way to improve the quality of life of someone on a fixed income. Others enhance their lifestyles by accessing home equity to pay for home upgrades, travel, or new vehicles.

3. A Reverse Mortgage as financial <u>PLAN</u>

Financial planners are now recommending Reverse Mortgages for clients who do not have an immediate need for them. Why? In part, because many homeowners have disproportionate amounts of their retirement savings held in real estate. Drawing part of their monthly cash flow (tax-free) from their home equity nest eggs will help their traditional retirement funds last much longer.

The primary financial planning advantage, however, is the available line-of-credit (LOC). This option allows homeowners to have an emergency fund that grows (again tax-free) at current interest rates. The funds can be easily converted to monthly cash flow later in retirement. Because the LOC experiences compounding growth, many homeowners will opt-in as early as possible (age 62), and draw their increased funds at a later date, as a form of tax-free retirement income.

Because the Reverse Mortgage has the ability to create this growing alternate source of retirement cash flow, a homeowner's Financial Planner will have the flexibility to manage his/her adjusted gross income for tax savings. More importantly, it can give homeowners peace of mind that they will be less likely to run out of funds.

Let's look at REFERENCES

HUD Handbook 4235.1 Chapter 1-2.
PURPOSE OF THE PROGRAM

The program insures what are commonly referred to as Reverse Mortgages, and is designed to enable elderly homeowners to convert the equity in their homes to monthly streams of income and/or lines of credit.

Chapter 3

When is a Reverse Mortgage
NOT A GOOD OPTION?

Reverse Mortgage Professionals find themselves constantly touting, defending, and pitching the numerous advantages of the federally insured Home Equity Conversion Mortgage (HECM). The primary reason they put forth so much effort is not to make a sale. It is because the public is still confused and largely unaware of the lifestyle and financial planning advantages of the product. After 27 years, many older homeowners still think they lose title and ownership of their homes with this financial tool.

However, most eligible candidates are ALSO unaware of the many real reasons NOT to get one. The fact is, there are individuals for whom this is not a good fit. It would be best to identify these candidates upfront before they spend the time, energy, and money it requires to complete the mandatory HECM counseling. So, let's highlight a few scenarios that could mean a Reverse Mortgage might not be a good option:

1. If the home does not fit
the homeowner's long-term needs
If the homeowner has the intention of selling the home within the short-term, or if the home does not meet their long-term physical needs, a Reverse Mortgage may not be a good fit. While

they can certainly sell the home at any time, the program was designed to meet the needs of older Americans who wish to age in place. If you want to stay, and are physically able to stay, you have passed my first test.

2. If the Reverse Mortgage does not provide a tangible benefit

It not only has to make sense right now, but also needs to provide a sustainable solution throughout retirement. If the Reverse Mortgage offers little current or future advantage to a borrower, then the homeowner should look for other options.

And using a Reverse Mortgage to eliminate monthly mortgage payments does not always guarantee that a homeowner will have positive monthly cash flow. New regulations, however, were implemented to ensure that monthly residual income is considered in underwriting Reverse Mortgages.

3. If the homeowner does not adequately understand the product

A HECM borrower or their trusted advisor must be comfortable paying property charges, maintaining the home, and managing finances. Unfortunately, many are not accustomed to handling these items. In addition, some have competency issues that prevent them from fully understanding the complex loan product for which they are applying. Consequently, HECM Counseling is required to make sure all parties understand not only the product, but also other options that may be available to them.

4. If the homeowner wishes to protect a legacy

I reluctantly include this item on the list. Many experts don't consider inheritance a reason NOT to get a Reverse Mortgage. This is because homeowners who obtain a growing HECM line-of-credit early in retirement are better equipped to decide how future expenses are paid—by the homeowner, by the heirs, or by the home.

Some homeowners, however, wish to protect their home's equity as a legacy for their heirs, and would never consider accessing home equity in an emergency. That's a very nice gesture, and I can understand wanting to leave an inheritance to loved ones. The question becomes whether an inheritance is a right of heirs, or a gift.

Let's look at REFERENCES

CFPB–Report to Congress or Reverse Mortgages (June 2012)

Meanwhile, if prospective borrowers do not have adequate savings and other retirement resources and are instead struggling to make ends meet, using a reverse mortgage to refinance an existing traditional mortgage can result in even greater long-term financial risk to the borrower. Some prospective borrowers' financial situations may be fundamentally unsustainable. Using a reverse mortgage to hold on to the home for the near term may simply postpone hard decisions, provide little long-term benefit to the borrower, and consume most or all of the borrower's home equity in the process. This type of borrower is at high risk of getting behind on taxes and insurance, and facing foreclosure on the reverse mortgage.

Chapter 4

What is a HECM or Home Equity Conversion Mortgage?

The Home Equity Conversion Mortgage (HECM) is the only Reverse Mortgage that is insured by the Federal Government. Because of their involvement, lenders can offer these non-recourse loans at low interest rates, and offer very generous financing terms. When I say "Federal Government," I am referring to HUD and FHA.

HUD: U.S. Department of Housing and Urban Development
FHA: Federal Housing Administration, a Division of HUD

They insure HECM loans, and along with the Consumer Financial Protection Bureau (CFPB), they regulate the HECM program.

HECMs have become increasingly attractive for the lender, the homeowner, the homeowner's heirs, and now for spouses of borrowers as well. Because of the HECM's popularity, few proprietary Reverse Mortgage products are available.

WHAT IS SO ATTRACTIVE ABOUT HECMS?
The Federal Housing Administration (FHA) offers the mortgage insurance with no profit margin built in. This means that the government is not intending to make any money by insuring them.

If a lender had to self-insure a non-recourse loan, the interest rates would have to be much higher. Otherwise, the lender would have to offer homeowners much less money.

WHAT ARE KEY ELIGIBILITY REQUIREMENTS FOR HECMS?

Lender guidelines may vary slightly. However, the key eligibility requirements remain the same; the youngest borrower must be at least 62, and they must own and occupy the property.

Age

The most important eligibility requirement may be that the borrower is age 62 or older. Most lenders will not begin the application process until the youngest borrower is at least 62. But age is only counted in whole years. Therefore, a borrower, age 69, who will turn 70 within 6 months of closing, is considered to be 70. The advantage here is that they will qualify for higher principal limits. However, that does not help a borrower age 61.5. Borrowers don't become eligible until they officially turn 62.

Homeownership

In order to qualify for a traditional HECM, one must not only be the homeowner, but also must have significant home equity. That is generally true. Some homeowners with little or no equity in their homes can still qualify for traditional HECMs. They are simply "short-to-close," meaning that they will be required to bring funds to closing.

With the HECM for Purchase program, a borrower will become a homeowner on the new property, and will be generating equity in the home by bringing funds to closing. This is often not a problem for an older adult who has just sold a property, probated the will of a parent, or liquidated an investment.

Residency

The home must be the homeowner's principal residence. This program is not available for second homes or investment properties. Of course this is something the lender will verify at origination. However, the HECM program also requires an annual certification that the homeowner still resides in the home.

Property Type

These guidelines may vary slightly from lender to lender, but the following list is generally accepted for eligible property types:

• Single Family Residence

• 2-4 unit property, as long as one unit is occupied by the borrower

• Town home

• Condo in a HUD-approved condominium project

• Planned Unit Development (PUD)

• Modular home

• Manufactured homes that meet FHA requirements

Let's look at REFERENCES
Section 255 of the National Housing Act
(12 U.S.C. 1715z–20)

The purpose of this section is to authorize the Secretary to carry out a program of mortgage insurance designed to meet the special needs of elderly homeowners by reducing the effect of the economic hardship caused by the increasing costs of meeting health, housing, and subsistence needs at a time of reduced income, through the insurance of home equity conversion mortgages to permit the conversion of a portion of accumulated home equity into liquid assets.

24 CFR § 206.33. AGE OF MORTGAGOR

The youngest mortgagor shall be 62 years of age or older at the time the mortgagee submits the application for insurance.

24 CFR § 206.39. PRINCIPAL RESIDENCE

The property must be the principal residence of each mortgagor at closing. For purposes of this section, the property will be considered to be the principal residence of any mortgagor who is temporarily or permanently in a health care institution as long as the property is the principal residence of at least one other mortgagor who is not in a health care institution.

24 CFR § 206.211. ANNUAL DETERMINATION
OF PRINCIPAL RESIDENCE

At least once during each calendar year, the mortgagee shall determine whether or not the property is the principal residence of at least one mortgagor. The mortgagee shall require each mortgagor to make an annual certification of his or her principal residence, and the mortgagee may rely on the certification unless it has information indicating that the certification may be false.

Chapter 5

What are

MANDATORY OBLIGATIONS?

Mandatory Obligations are items that must be paid off at closing. These generally include mortgages against the property, liens, judgments that affect the owner's title, federal debt, closing costs, initial mortgage insurance premiums, etc. The vast majority of borrowers finance these items into the loan. As a result, the homeowner generally does not "pay" these until the home sells.

The homeowner's available funds are often referred to as the net principal limit, and this is what is available after mandatory obligations have been paid. One way to describe this is shown here:

Principal Limit – Mandatory Obligations
= Net Principal Limit

Historically, borrowers have been required (on fixed rate loans) or encouraged (on ARMs) to take 100% of their net principal limit at the time the loan closes. As a result, many homeowners were borrowing funds they did not necessarily need. These were also higher risk loans for FHA, because the borrower had drawn all of their available funds, and did not leave equity in reserve.

Because of the increased risks to FHA, HUD made changes in September of 2013. Some homeowners are STILL able to receive their one-time funds upfront. However, they are restricted to the greater of:

60% of the Principal Limit or
Mandatory Obligations + 10% of the PL

This is called the borrower's "Initial Disbursement Limit," and identifies the amount of funds available for the homeowner to draw at closing on a fixed rate HECM or during the first 12 months on an adjustable rate HECM. On the HECM-ARM, the remaining principal limit (plus growth) may be available to the borrower after the first year.

So, can a borrower get 100% of their principal limit? Absolutely, if their mandatory obligations are high enough. But they can't access MORE than 100%, as the principal limit is TRULY a LIMIT.

Let's look at EXAMPLES

WILLIAM has mandatory obligations that are 20% of his principal limit. He can then take up to 40% more of his principal limit in cash allowance. That would total 60% of his principal limit.

SUSAN has mandatory obligations that are 55% of her principal limit. She can choose to take up to 5% of her principal limit in cash (total 60%), or take her 10% cash allowance (total 65%.)

RICHARD has mandatory obligations that are 90% of his principal limit. He can still take 10% of his principal limit in cash. That would total 100% of his principal limit.

Let's look at REFERENCES

Mortgagee Letter 2013-27. INITIAL DISBURSEMENT LIMITS

Mandatory Obligations for Traditional and Refinance Transactions
Mandatory Obligations include: initial MIP, loan origination fee, HECM counseling, recording fees and recording taxes, credit report, survey, title examination, mortgagee's title insurance, fees paid to an appraiser for the initial appraisal of the property, repair administration fee, delinquent Federal debt, amounts required to discharge any existing liens on the property, customary fees and charges for warranties, inspections, surveys, engineer certifications, funds to pay contractors who performed repairs as a condition of closing, in accordance with standard FHA requirements for repairs required by appraiser, and other charges as authorized by the Secretary.

Mortgagee Letter 2013-33. MANDATORY OBLIGATIONS

Mandatory Obligations for Traditional and Refinance Transactions
In addition to those items announced in Mortgagee Letter 2013-27, Mandatory Obligations also include: Repair Set-Asides, and Property Tax, Flood and Hazard Insurance payments required by the Mortgagee to be paid at closing.

Chapter 6

What do you mean a Reverse Mortgage is NON-RECOURSE?

The non-recourse feature ranks up there with the line-of credit as one of the two most powerful aspects of a Reverse Mortgage. The homeowner is not responsible for mortgage debt that accrues beyond the home's value. If property values drop, or if one or both homeowners live a very long time, this feature can give the homeowners the peace of mind that they will not be leaving their heirs with a bill.

The abbreviated definition of "NON-RECOURSE" is that "THE **HOME** STANDS FOR THE DEBT"…NOT the home-owner and not their heirs. Another succinct way of expressing this is "there is NO RECOURSE for any mortgage loan deficiency other than the home."

However, the proper definition of the non-recourse feature is:

"FHA guarantees that the borrower will not owe more than the home is worth at the time it is sold"

This should be comforting to every homeowner and their heirs. They can be assured that if a homeowner lives a very long time, or if property values drop, FHA will pay a claim to the lender so that nobody is harmed by the loan being "upside down" or "under water."

Before you say this is too good to be true, this is why FHA collects mortgage insurance premiums. FHA's Mutual Mortgage Insurance Fund (MMIF) is a pool of funds created for this purpose. This is a primary consumer protection that makes HECMs so attractive.

First, let's clarify that the loan balance technically CAN exceed the home's value. The lender is not ordering appraisals periodically and turning off the interest accruals. The homeowner is simply not responsible for the amount that exceeds the home's value when the home is sold.

Non-Recourse

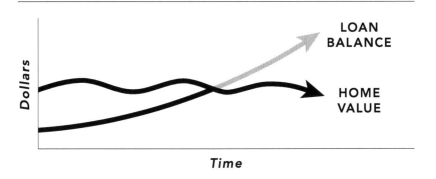

The chart above shows how the loan balance may exceed the home's value if home values do not appreciate as expected. In these cases, the non-recourse feature is quite advantageous.

In fact, after the last borrower has died, the property may be sold for 95% of the home's value, and again there is no recourse to the estate.

Let's look at an EXAMPLE

Mary has a Reverse Mortgage, and had $75,000 equity in her home at the beginning of her loan. However, this can change. Mary's loan balance will rise, as it is accruing interest. If she lives a long time, takes future draws, or if her home value declines, she may eventually have a loan balance that exceeds her home value as shown below.

		BEGINNING		SOMETIME IN THE FUTURE
Home Value		$200,000	declines to	$150,000
Loan Balance		$125,000	rises to	$200,000
Home Equity	=	$75,000	=	-$50,000
				(non-recourse)

As you can see, Mary's home value declined at the same time that her loan balance grew. Her equity position changed as a result. She had $75,000 in equity at the start, but it eventually became $50,000 upside down.

If Mary is upside down at the time she wishes to sell, as shown in the second column **(-$50,000),** she or her heirs would have the opportunity to sell the home for the new home value of $150,000 despite being upside down. And it is possible that when Mary passes away, the home may be sold for $142,500, which is 95% of the home's value, with no negative consequences for the estate.

Let's look at REFERENCES

24 CFR § 206.27. MORTGAGE PROVISIONS

The mortgagor shall have no personal liability for payment of the mortgage balance. The mortgagee shall enforce the debt only through sale of the property. The mortgagee shall not be permitted to obtain a deficiency judgment against the mortgagor if the mortgage is foreclosed.

HUD Handbook 4235.1 Chapter 1-3. NON-RECOURSE

The HECM is a non-recourse loan. This means that the HECM borrower (or his or her estate) will never owe more than the loan balance or value of the property, whichever is less; and no assets other than the home must be used to repay the debt.

Chapter 7

Will the Reverse Mortgage
STICK MY HEIRS WITH A BILL?

No. Fortunately, this is where FHA's insurance kicks in. As we saw in the previous section Reverse Mortgages are non-recourse loans. But the main impact of this feature is that the homeowners, and their heirs, have no obligation to pay for any deficiency caused by the home being worth less than the loan balance.

Another way to describe this is that the home may be sold for the lesser of the mortgage balance or the home's value.

Let's look at an EXAMPLE

James takes a Reverse Mortgage at age 78 at 5.25%. That would give him principal limit factors of 61%. With a home worth $300,000, he is able to access up to $183,000 to pay-off his mandatory obligations.

James is not required to make payments. However, because he doesn't, his mortgage balance may be $350,000 after ten years. During this time, his home value appreciates temporarily, but then loses value to finish back at $300,000 at the time he passes away.

(continued)

> His heirs are NOT stuck with a bill for $50,000 to satisfy the difference between James' home value and loan balance. In fact, the heirs could walk away from the property or obtain the home for 95% of the home's value ($285,000.)

Generally, the heirs will sell the home when the last surviving borrower passes away. The Reverse Mortgage balance is paid off at closing just like any other lien, and the remainder would be a form of inheritance for them.

However, if the home is worth less than the loan balance, the deficiency is paid through the Mutual Mortgage Insurance Fund so that the lender, investor, borrower, and the borrower's heirs are not stuck with a bill.

Let's look at REFERENCES

HUD Communication to All HUD-Approved
Housing Counseling Agencies 6/12/13

HUD's regulations at 24 CFR 206.125(c) state, in part, that "[i]f the mortgage is due and payable at the time the contract for sale is executed, the borrower may sell the property for at least the lesser of the mortgage balance or five percent under the appraised value" (i.e., 95% of the appraised value of the mortgaged property). HUD interprets the word "sale" to include any post-death conveyance of the mortgage property (even by operation of law) to the borrower's estate or heirs (including a surviving spouse who is not obligated on the HECM note). A loan payoff that occurs simultaneously with or immediately following such a post-death conveyance will be regarded as a sale transaction for purposes of section 206.125(c).

HUD.GOV—
HECM Servicing Frequently Asked Questions (FAQs)

When a HECM loan becomes due and payable as a result of the mortgagor's death and the property is conveyed by will or operation of law to the mortgagor's estate or heirs, that party may satisfy the HECM debt by paying the lesser of the mortgage balance or 95% of the current appraised value of the property."

Chapter 8

What are MATURITY EVENTS
that cause the loan to be due?

An important criteria to understand is that at least one borrower must occupy the home as their principal residence. Therefore, the death of one borrower does not cause the loan to mature. In fact, borrowers may move out, or move into assisted living, as long as at least one borrower still occupies the home. Even after the death of the last borrower, a non-borrowing spouse may continue to occupy the home with a deferral of the "due and payable" status despite not being on the home's title or on the loan.

HECM loans mature when certain specific events occur. These are called "Maturity Events," and these may cause HECMs to become due and payable. Loan Maturity occurs when:

- **The property is no longer the principal residence of at least one borrower.** This could result from the last surviving borrower passing away or abandoning the home.

- **The last borrower fails to occupy the property for 12 consecutive months because of mental or physical illness.** One year is considered to be permanently vacating the home.

- **A borrower does not fulfill their obligations under the terms of the loan.** Failure to maintain the home in good condition or failure to pay property taxes, property insurance, or other property charges are common examples.

These, however, do not necessarily cause the loan to become due and payable. FHA has allowed the "due and payable" status of a HECM to be deferred under certain conditions when a non-borrowing spouse is involved.

If a non-borrowing spouse is still occupying the home, they may have additional rights under new guidelines that went into effect Aug. 4, 2014. Reference the section in this book titled, "What if my spouse is not 62 or older."

The borrower (or the heirs if the borrower has passed away) will need to notify the lender that a maturity event has occurred. They then have multiple options outlined in the previous chapter. However, the heirs generally:

- **Sell the home**
- **Repay the loan balance, or**
- **Refinance the home**

In each of these three scenarios, the borrowers and the heirs have the protection of the non-recourse feature. In fact, the heirs may also be able to sell or buy the home for the lesser of the Mortgage Balance or 95% of appraised value.

Let's look at REFERENCES
HUD Handbook 4235.1 Chapter 1-13.
RECOVERY OF MORTGAGE PROCEEDS
The borrower may occupy the property until the mortgage becomes due and payable. A mortgage will become due and payable when the borrower dies, the property is no longer the borrower's principal residence, the borrower does not occupy the property for 12 consecutive months for health reasons, or the borrower violates the mortgage covenants.

When the mortgage becomes due and payable, the property will normally be sold by the borrower or the borrower's estate to pay off the outstanding balance on the mortgage.

Since a HECM is a non-recourse loan, the lender's recovery from the borrower will be limited to the value of the home. There will be no deficiency judgment taken against the borrower or the estate because there is no personal liability for payment of the loan balance.

24 CFR § 206.27. MORTGAGE PROVISIONS
Date the mortgage comes due and payable.
The mortgage shall state that the mortgage balance will be due and payable in full if a mortgagor dies and the property is not the principal residence of at least one surviving mortgagor, or a mortgagor conveys all or his or her title in the property and no other mortgagor retains title to the property. For purposes of the preceding sentence, a mortgagor retains title in the property if the mortgagor continues to hold title to any part of the property in fee simple, as a leasehold interest as set forth in § 206.45(a), or as a life estate.

The mortgage shall state that the mortgage balance shall be due and payable in full, upon approval of the Secretary, if any of the following occur:

(i) The property ceases to be the principal residence of a mortgagor for reasons other than death and the property is not the principal residence of at least one other mortgagor;

(ii) For a period of longer than 12 consecutive months, a mortgagor fails to occupy the property because of physical or mental illness and the property is not the principal residence of at least one other mortgagor; or

(iii) An obligation of the mortgagor under the mortgage is not performed.

Chapter 9

How is my
PRINCIPAL LIMIT calculated?

This happens to be one of the most common questions I get. Many lenders have HECM calculators on their websites which ask for basic information. The calculators process this data and generate principal limits that are generally consistent from lender to lender. But most homeowners and many mortgage brokers are unaware of how the figure is actually calculated.

Principal limits are determined by referencing principal limit factor (PLF) tables of relevant ages and expected rates (ER). For every **age** from 18 to 99 combined with an **expected rate** between 3% and 18.875%, there is a PLF shown as a percentage.

PLF tables change periodically, but the following diagram is a way to describe the process:

Principal Limit Factors

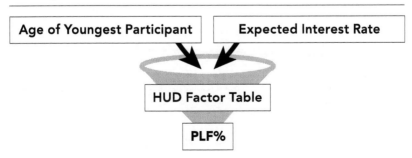

As you can see, we are using the age of the "youngest participant," which is the term I use to describe the youngest borrower, co-borrower, or non-borrowing spouse.

Using these two items, we can look up a PLF from HUD's Factor Table. In the chart below, you will see a small sample of selected ages and selected expected rates.

PLFs for Selected Ages and Rates

Expected Interest Rates

Age	5.00%	5.25%	5.50%
70	57.6%	54.4%	51.3%
71	58.3%	55.2%	52.1%
72	59.1%	56.0%	52.9%
73	59.8%	56.8%	53.7%
74	60.6%	57.5%	54.5%
75	61.4%	58.3%	55.3%

When the PLF% is multiplied by the homeowner's maximum claim amount (MCA = the lesser of home value or $636,150), we get the principal limit in dollars.

Let's look at an EXAMPLE

Linda is 74 years old, and she is younger than her spouse. Therefore, she is the youngest participant. She has been quoted a rate of 5.00%. Using these two pieces of information, we can look up a PLF of 60.6%.

60.6% of Linda's home value of $200,000 will give her a principal limit of $121,200.

Historically, the principal limit has been a measure of what HUD says a borrower with certain factors is able to borrow at closing. After the September 2013 changes to the program, however, that definition is not quite accurate. Homeowners may be restricted in the amounts they can borrow up-front. Fortunately, with the adjustable rate products, the remaining net principal limit will be accessible after that first year.

Let's look at REFERENCES

HUD Handbook 4235.1 Chapter 1-4. PRINCIPAL LIMIT

The amount that the borrower can receive from a Reverse Mortgage is determined by calculating the principal limit. The figure increases monthly and represents the maximum payment that a borrower may receive. The principal limit at origination is based on the age of the youngest borrower, the expected average mortgage interest rate, and the maximum claim amount.

Chapter 10

What happens to
THE HOME when I die?

There are a few misconceptions that have persisted from a time before Reverse Mortgages became regulated and federally-insured financial tools. Correcting these fallacies has been an uphill battle. Many in the industry are passionate about the advantages of this program, and have tried to offer a correct understanding.

No. The lender does NOT get the home, take title to the home, or own the home or its equity in any way. In fact, a homeowner or heir can sell the home with no prepayment penalties. The HECM is simply a lien. When they sell the home, the Reverse Mortgage lien is paid off just like any other lien would be paid off.

We will discuss later in this book what happens if a non-borrowing spouse (NBS) is still occupying the home. However, at this moment, let's assume that is not the case. So, then, what DOES happen when the last surviving borrower passes way?

At that time, the heirs have multiple options. These options are easily revealed when the heirs answer these two primary questions: **"Does the loan balance exceed the home value?" and "Do I want to keep the home?"**

Options for Heirs

Is the home upside down?

Do you want the home?		YES	NO
	YES	(1.) 95% (Non-Recourse)	(2.) Payoff or Refinance
	NO	(3.) Deed-in-Lieu (Non-Recourse)	(4.) Sell the Home (Inheritance)

If the heirs want to keep the home, they can:

(1.) **Obtain the home for 95% of the current home value.** The non-recourse feature protects the heirs' interests in a post-death conveyance (transfer) of the property.

(2.) **Pay off the mortgage balance.** This generally requires the heirs to refinance the full outstanding loan balance.

If the heirs do not want the home, they can:

(3.) **Sign a Deed-in-Lieu of Foreclosure.** If there is no economic value to selling the home, the heirs can relinquish the home to the lender/servicer. The non-recourse feature is an advantage to the heirs because there is no recourse for any deficiency caused by the loan balance exceeding the home's value.

(4.) **Sell the home and receive a gain on the sale.** This is a very common way the borrowers are able to pass on an inheritance to their heirs.

If the heirs wish to sell the home, they must first notify the servicer. They will then have six months to sell the home. During this time, they are not required to pay any monthly principal and interest payments, and they may have up to two 90-day extensions that are generally HUD-approved.

Let's look at REFERENCES
24 CFR § 206.125a. ACQUISITION AND SALE OF THE PROPERTY.

After notifying the Secretary, and receiving approval of the Secretary when needed, the mortgagee shall notify the mortgagor that the mortgage is due and payable, unless the mortgage is due and payable by reason of the mortgagor's death. The mortgagee shall require the mortgagor to

(i) pay the mortgage balance, including any accrued interest and MIP, in full;

(ii) sell the property for at least 95% of the appraised value as determined under § 206.125(b), with the net proceeds of the sale to be applied towards the mortgage balance; or

(iii) provide the mortgagee with a deed in lieu of foreclosure. The mortgagor shall have 30 days in which to comply with the preceding sentence, or correct the matter which resulted in the mortgage coming due and payable, before a foreclosure proceeding is begun.

Chapter 11

How much HOME EQUITY

do I need?

The more appropriate question is, **"how much home equity do I need <u>so that I don't need to bring money to closing?"</u>** A homeowner can owe more than their home is worth, sometimes described as being "upside-down," and STILL qualify for a HECM. They would simply need to bring funds to closing in those cases. When the principal limit is not sufficient to cover all of the homeowner's mandatory obligations, we call this "short to close," and many such borrowers are willing to bring funds to closing in those cases. A borrower with a $2,000 monthly forward mortgage payment that is only $1,000 short to close on a Reverse Mortgage would be a good example. For just a portion (one-half) of the next scheduled payment, the borrower may obtain the Reverse Mortgage and not have to make monthly principal and interest mortgage payments any longer.

We know that the amount for which a homeowner can qualify (principal limit) will be impacted by the relevant age and interest rates. However, we are not sure about the home's value until an appraisal is complete. So, at application, we cannot tell precisely how much equity a homeowner might have, and whether they are short to close.

When we know the homeowner's principal limit, we can then use the following formula:

Principal Limit
(This represents the homeowner's accessible funds.)

– Mandatory Obligations
(These are items that must be paid off at closing.)

= Net Principal Limit
(This is what is left over.)

Let's look at an EXAMPLE

John has a home value of $200,000, and qualifies for a principal limit factor (PLF) of 60%. This means he has an initial principal limit (PL) of $120,000. John has mandatory obligations (mortgage payoffs and closing costs) totaling $100,000.

$120,000	Principal Limit
– $100,000	Mandatory Obligations
= $20,000	Net Principal Limit

John has equity in his home. This $20,000, however, represents the portion of John's equity that may be accessible with a HECM after paying his mandatory obligations.

Chapter 12

What is

FINANCIAL ASSESSMENT?

The federally insured Reverse Mortgage program went through another major change effective April 27, 2015 called "Financial Assessment." At that time, Reverse Mortgage lenders were required to begin assessing each borrower's credit history, property charge history, and monthly residual income. This was a dramatic change for an industry where the focus had been primarily on the value of a home.

WHY FINANCIAL ASSESSMENT?

The first question many asked was, "why does credit matter when originating a loan that doesn't require monthly principal and interest payments?" After all, the value of the home and the age of the borrower are the primary factors in qualifying. So, why are credit and residual income now included in the underwriting of these loans?

The answer is that Reverse Mortgages MUST be a sustainable solution for each homeowner. Ideally, Reverse Mortgages should always leave the borrower with the ability to pay their property charges and monthly bills in the future.

The reality is that the HECM may not be the proper solution for some borrowers, and the most prudent way to document sustainability is with an assessment of each borrower's credit report, property charge history, and residual income.

According to Mortgagee Letter 2014-21, "The mortgagee (lender) must evaluate the mortgagor's (borrower's) willingness and capacity to timely meet his or her financial obligations and to comply with the mortgage requirements."

The critical borrower obligations and mortgage requirements are as follows:

- **Upkeep of the home in good condition**

- **Payment of property taxes**

- **Payment of homeowners insurance**

- **Payment of other property charges (flood insurance, HOA dues, condo dues, etc.)**

These are FHA requirements, and lenders must document every borrower's ability to meet these obligations.

It is important to note, however, that Financial Assessment is NOT necessarily a "yes or no" qualification of the borrower. The results of a Financial Assessment are generally used to determine if funds need to be set aside to ensure property charges are paid in the future.

WHO PERFORMS FINANCIAL ASSESSMENT?

The lender's underwriter will perform two tests, a credit and property charge payment test and a residual income test. If the underwriter determines that one or both of the financial assessment tests don't meet FHA requirements, a Life Expectancy Set-Aside (or LESA) will be required.

WHAT IS A LIFE EXPECTANCY SET-ASIDE (LESA)?

When the underwriter determines that one or more of the financial assessment tests have failed, a Life Expectancy Set-Aside (or LESA) will be required. These are funds that are removed from the borrower's principal limit and set aside for the purpose of paying property charges over a calculated time period. The two types of LESAs that may be required are described here:

Fully-Funded LESA:

The lender uses funds set-aside from the borrower's principal limit to pay three critical property charges; property taxes, homeowners insurance, and flood insurance (if needed). The lender pays these charges directly when the bills are due, in the same way a traditional escrow account functions.

Partially-Funded LESA:

The lender uses funds set-aside from the borrower's principal limit to supplement the borrower's income. This is done to fund a home-owner's gap in residual income. The lender releases necessary funds to the borrower semi-annually. The borrower, however, will be responsible for paying their own property charges.

WHAT ARE EXTENUATING CIRCUMSTANCES AND COMPENSATING FACTORS?

Extenuating Circumstances are explanations for credit imperfections. This will require a formal letter of explanation from the borrower. Then an underwriter will determine whether this can offset any derogatory credit.

Compensating Factors are items that an underwriter will evaluate that may compensate for low residual income. An example may be large assets that the borrower could sell in the future if needed.

HOW DO WE KNOW WHICH LESA TO USE?

The appropriate set-aside is determined by looking at the answers to these 2 critical questions:

---

1. **Does the borrower have acceptable CREDIT and PROPERTY CHARGE HISTORY?**

   If **NO,** then barring any extenuating circumstances, the borrower will need a Fully-Funded Life Expectancy Set-Aside (LESA).

   If **YES,** move on to Question #2.

2. **Does the borrower have acceptable monthly RESIDUAL INCOME?**

   If **NO,** then barring any extenuating circumstances, the borrower will need a Partially-Funded Life Expectancy Set-Aside (LESA).

   If **YES,** then no LESA is needed.

There are 2 exceptions to the rules listed above, which may cause a Partially-Funded LESA to revert to a Fully-Funded LESA.

The 75% Exception

Where the projected Partially Funded LESA is greater than 75% of the Fully Funded LESA, the mortgagor is not eligible for the Partially Funded LESA. In other words, if the borrower's gap in residual income is that large, FHA would rather make sure the property charges are directly paid (fully funded) by the lender.

Fixed Rate Loan Exception

Fixed rate loans are closed-ended loans, meaning the lender cannot make future distributions (Partially Funded) to a borrower after closing. So, the Fully-Funded LESA will be required for all Fixed Rate HECMs that require a set-aside.

Remember, Financial Assessment is NOT necessarily designed to be a "yes or no" qualification of a borrower. However, if homeowners do not have sufficient equity to set-aside funds for future property charges, they may not qualify for the program.

On one hand, fewer homeowners now qualify for Reverse Mortgages. On the other hand, those who do qualify are better equipped to stay in their homes, while the lender and the federal government maintain higher quality loans.

Let's look at REFERENCES

Mortgagee Letter 2014-21. CREDIT HISTORY ANALYSIS

Mortgagees must perform a credit history analysis, in accordance with FHA guidelines, for each prospective mortgagor to determine if the mortgagor has demonstrated the willingness to meet their financial obligations by analyzing each mortgagor's credit and property charge history.

Mortgagee Letter 2014-21. RESIDUAL INCOME ANALYSIS

Mortgagees must perform a cash flow/residual income analysis, in accordance with FHA guidelines, to determine the capacity of the mortgagor to meet his or her documented financial obligations with his or her documented income.

HECM Financial Assessment and Property Charge Guide (Revised July 13, 2016)

Through the Fully Funded LESA the mortgagee will use HECM proceeds to pay property taxes and insurance premiums on behalf of the mortgagor. The mortgagor remains responsible for all other property charges.

Through the Partially-Funded LESA the mortgagor will receive semi-annual payments from HECM proceeds to be used to pay property taxes and insurance premiums. The mortgagor remains responsible for timely payment of all property charges.

Chapter 13

What are my
PRODUCT OPTIONS?

There has been a debate in the industry about whether the HECM is two products; a fixed rate product and an adjustable rate (ARM) product, or whether the HECM is one product with two rate options, each with different payout guidelines.

HECM-Fixed vs. HECM-ARM

Either way, the HECM-Fixed is popular because the rate stability is attractive to many borrowers. It is nice to not have to worry about rising interest rates. Meanwhile, the currently low interest rates and payout options on the ARMs are compelling for others.

FIXED RATE
(Single Disbursement Lump Sum Payment)
Fixed rate HECM products have only been around for a few years, and they are closed-end loans. "Closed-End" means the borrower receives all of their proceeds when the loan closes. These loans are not "Open," so to speak, for future draws. With the changes to the loan program in September 2013, the homeowner is no longer required to draw all of the funds for which they qualify. However, those changes also stipulate that the

MAXIMUM the borrower can receive at closing (Disbursement Limit) will be the greater of the following two amounts:

Option 1:
60% of the borrower's Principal Limit, or

Option 2:
Their Mandatory Obligations plus 10% (cash allowance)

As a single-disbursement loan, the borrower would NOT be eligible for future draws. Any funds the borrower wishes to receive must be taken at the time of closing. Therefore, this fixed rate option is also known as a "Single Disbursement Lump Sum Payment" option.

Let's look at an EXAMPLE

David has a home valued at 190,000 and based on his age, and fixed interest rate, he qualifies for a principal limit of $100,000.

Option 1: If David has little (or no) mortgage liens to pay off, he could receive his Single Disbursement Lump Sum Payment of up to $60,000…and no more.

Option 2: However, if David needs the $100,000 to pay off his mandatory obligations, his Single Disbursement Lump Sum Payment of up to $100,000 may be utilized. This will also be his beginning loan balance.

Because this is a closed-end loan, David can pay down his balance at any time, but he does not have the ability to take future draws.

ADJUSTABLE RATE

The HECM-ARM is a different animal altogether. It is "Open Ended," and it allows for multiple payout options that are quite flexible. Ultimately, it allows the user to get much more from their HECM, and has many financial planning advantages that will be discussed later.

Let's first discuss what "Open-End" means for a HECM. Open-End credit allows the borrower to take future draws, and make payments that increase future borrowing capacity. Therefore, making payments toward an adjustable rate HECM loan balance will not only reduce the loan balance, but will boost the borrower's line of credit for future use.

The Initial Disbursement Limits work differently for the HECM-ARM. Instead of limiting draws to closing day, the ARMs allow the borrower the option of utilizing the greater of the following two amounts during the first year:

Option 1:
60% of the borrower's Principal Limit, or

Option 2:
Their Mandatory Obligations plus 10% (cash allowance)

The advantage over the fixed rate product is that borrowers may access the remainder of their principal limit (plus growth) at any time after the first year, when the Initial Disbursement Period ends.

> ## Let's look at an EXAMPLE
>
> Deborah has a home valued at $200,000 and based on her age and expected interest rate, she qualifies for a principal limit of $120,000.
>
> **Option 1:** If Deborah has little (or no) mortgage liens to pay off, she could utilize up to the 60% threshold ($72,000) during the first year, after which the remaining principal limit ($48,000 plus growth) would become available.
>
> **Option 2:** However, if Deborah needs $110,000 to pay off her mandatory obligations and $10,000 in cash, she may be able to utilize the full $120,000 during the first year.
>
> Because this is an open-ended loan, Deborah can pay down her balance at any time. This may boost her line of credit, and will offer her a greater capacity to take future draws.

The most important factor in choosing a fixed rate or adjustable rate option is NOT the rate itself. It is which PAYOUT OPTION best fits the homeowner's needs. The payout options the homeowner has will depend on whether the HECM is a fixed rate or adjustable rate product.

PROPRIETARY PRODUCTS

Proprietary loan products are privately funded and not government insured. Some homeowners in certain markets may find these loan programs may be beneficial. I have trained brokers on the guidelines for jumbo Reverse Mortgage products in the past. However, because the guidelines for these are quite different, it would be best to contact an experienced Reverse Mortgage Professional in your area for more specifics.

Let's look at REFERENCES ————————

24 CFR § 206.17

Interest rate. A mortgage shall provide for either fixed or adjustable interest rates in accordance with § 206.21.

24 CFR § 206.21. INTEREST RATE.

Fixed interest rate. A fixed interest rate is agreed upon by the mortgagor and mortgagee.

Adjustable interest rate. An initial interest rate is agreed upon by the mortgagor and mortgagee. The interest rate shall be adjusted in one of two ways depending on the option selected by the mortgagor. Whenever an interest rate is adjusted, the new interest rate applies to the entire mortgage balance. The difference between the initial interest rate and the index figure applicable when the firm commitment is issued shall equal the margin used to determine interest rate adjustments.

**Mortgagee Letter 2013-27 SINGLE
DISBURSEMENT LUMP SUM PAYMENT**

The maximum disbursement allowed at loan closing is: The greater of:

- sixty percent (60%) of the Principal Limit; or
- the sum of Mandatory Obligations plus ten percent of the Principal Limit.

Note: The combination of Mandatory Obligations, Set Asides and other charges will reduce the amount of funds available to the mortgagor. The Initial Disbursement Limit can only be taken at the time of loan closing.

Chapter 14

What are my PAYOUT OPTIONS?

As you can see from the previous chapter, the fixed rate HECM and the adjustable rate HECM are quite different in their payout possibilities. Fixed rate HECMs serve a purpose, but are only available as a Single Disbursement Lump Sum Payment. The adjustable rate (ARM) option is much more flexible. Let's give you a little more detail on the payout options available to homeowners.

WITH A HECM-FIXED
Single Disbursement Lump Sum Payment ONLY
This is easiest to explain by revisiting the Initial Disbursement Limits from the previous chapter. Just know that "Single Disbursement" means a one-time draw at the time of closing, and future draws are NOT permitted.

WITH A HECM-ARM
While adjustable rate HECM payouts have varied options, payments may be restricted during the first twelve months of the loan. It will be common for the line of credit to be restricted during the initial disbursement period. In addition, there will also be conditions where a monthly payment will be reduced for the first year to prevent the borrower from exceeding the 60% principal limit usage threshold. Rest assured, the remaining funds will be available on day 366.

Initial Draw

This is initial cash drawn at the time of closing. These funds, however, are not available until funding, which is ordinarily after the three-day rescission period ends. Nevertheless, we call this an "Initial Draw" because the ARM product allows for future draws.

Line of Credit (LOC)

This is the most popular payout option for multiple reasons. An open line allows a borrower to repay a portion of their loan balance and borrow it back again as needed. It also does not accrue interest and mortgage insurance on the amount that is left in the line. These two items are generally true of other traditional (forward) lines of credit as well. However, the HECM LOC also provides two major advantages that are NOT common to traditional lines of credit:

- **The available funds are secured.** The HECM line of credit is not capped, restricted, frozen, or eliminated if property values decline.

- **The available funds will grow.** The available LOC will grow with each payment to reduce the unpaid principal balance. In addition the available LOC grows at the compounding rate.

I'll spend an entire section later in the book explaining more about LOC growth, because it is one of the most powerful arguments for obtaining a Reverse Mortgage.

Tenure Payment

The word "TENURE" means "Permanent." In this payout structure, the borrower's net principal limit may be converted in a monthly draw that endures. These payments will continue as long as one or more borrowers occupy the home and follow program guidelines.

When explaining this option over the phone, I
a "d" at the end, to call them "tenured" payments ((
payments). This is because I have many clients misur
thinking I am explaining a "ten-year" program.

Term Payment

This can be a good option if the calculated tenure payment is
too small and more funds are needed on a monthly basis. Term
payments can be higher, but they are not permanent. They are
consistent monthly draws for a period of time; a specific number
of months. Shorter terms will provide larger payments, while
longer terms will provide smaller payments.

Imagine taking the homeowner's net principal limit and drawing
it all in six monthly payments. The payments would be relatively
large when compared to drawing equal monthly payments
for 20 years.

After the term period ends, the Reverse Mortgage is still active.
The borrower can still occupy the home, and the loan does
not have to be repaid as long as they continue to follow the
program guidelines.

Modified Tenure and Modified Term

"Modified," for this purpose, can be defined as a combination
of a monthly payment with a line of credit. A "modified tenure,"
therefore, is a tenure payment that has been adjusted to provide
the homeowner with a line of credit. A "modified term" is
a term payment that has been adjusted to provide the homeowner
with an LOC.

If the homeowner wants a $25,000 line of credit established
along with a monthly payment, the regular monthly draw
will decrease. The primary advantage is that the available line
of credit offers more flexibility and LOC growth that the homeowner would not have received with a pure monthly payment.

Let's look at REFERENCES ────────────
HUD Handbook 4235.1 Chapter 5-3. PAYMENT PLANS

The borrower can choose from among five different payment plans. The lender may not establish a minimum monthly payment or line of credit draw.

Tenure. The borrower may receive fixed monthly payments as long as he or she maintains the property as a principal residence.

Term. The borrower may receive fixed monthly payments for a term of months selected by the borrower, as long as he or she maintains the property as a principal residence.

Line of Credit. The borrower may elect to make withdrawals at times and in amounts of his or her choosing, as long as he or she maintains the property as a principal residence.

Modified Tenure. The borrower may combine a tenure payment plan (fixed monthly payments for as long as property is principal residence) with a line of credit. The borrower sets aside a portion of the principal limit as a line of credit from which to draw at times and in amounts of his or her choosing and receives the rest in equal monthly payments for as long as he or she continues to occupy the home as a principal residence.

Modified Term. The borrower may combine a term payment plan (fixed monthly payments for a term of months) with a line of credit. The borrower sets aside a portion of the principal limit as a line of credit from which to draw at times and in amounts of his or her choosing and receives the rest in equal monthly payments for a term of months selected by the borrower, as long as he or she maintains the property as a principal residence.

24 CFR § 206.19. PAYMENT OPTIONS

Term payment option. Under the term payment option, equal monthly payments are made by the mortgagee to the mortgagor for a fixed term of months chosen by the mortgagor, unless the mortgage is prepaid in full or becomes due and payable earlier under § 206.27(c).

Tenure payment option. Under the tenure payment option, equal monthly payments are made by the mortgagee to the mortgagor as long as the property is the principal residence of the mortgagor, unless the mortgage is prepaid in full or becomes due and payable under § 206.27(c).

Line of credit payment option. Under the line of credit payment option, payments are made by the mortgagee to the mortgagor at times and in amounts determined by the mortgagor as long as the amounts do not exceed the payment amounts permitted by § 206.25(d).

Chapter 15

Are HECMs EXPENSIVE?

That is a really good question and may be the toughest in the book to answer. I won't dodge the question, but I simply don't have the necessary information to determine whether or not it will be expensive for the homeowner. I often answer with "expensive compared to what?" Can it be compared to Long-term Care Insurance? Yes. Can it be viewed as insurance against home value declines? Yes. Can it even generate income? Yes, but it is much more than that. It is unique. There are no other financial tools like it.

Putting all of that to the side for a moment, the real question behind the question is "as a MORTGAGE, is it expensive?" In order to respond somewhat accurately, I would need to know the following:

1. How much will the home appreciate?
2. How long will the homeowner keep the HECM?
3. How much will the homeowner draw now
   and in the future?

But, wait a minute. Why does #1 matter? How does the home appreciation impact how expensive a HECM is? Because, if the home appreciates slowly, or not at all, or even depreciates, it is more likely the non-recourse feature will protect the homeowner. When the home value is less than the loan balance, the homeowner is not responsible for the additional interest and mortgage insurance that accrues above the home's value. In other words, if the home doesn't appreciate, a HECM can be very **INEXPENSIVE.**

Let's look at an EXAMPLE

Thomas' home was valued at $200,000 ten years ago when he got a Reverse Mortgage. He borrowed $120,000 over those ten years. During that time, his loan balance rose to $200,000, but his home value declined to $120,000. If Thomas were to sell the home right now, at market value, he would have borrowed $120,000 and paid back the same because of the non-recourse feature. Effectively, his real rate of interest would have been 0%. He borrowed and paid back the same amount. This is very inexpensive for Thomas, but rather unfortunate for FHA, who holds the insurance for this loan.

But let's get back to #2. A homeowner that holds a HECM for a short period of time will find this loan to be very **EXPENSIVE.** Imagine rolling $5,000 in closing costs into the loan balance, only to hold the loan for just one year. That can be viewed as an annual cost of $5,000 without even calculating the interest and mortgage insurance accruals. However, with the same closing costs spread over 20 years, it can be viewed as an annual cost of $250 per year. Longer terms show the mortgage to be much less expensive when viewed as a Total Annual Loan Cost.

#3 asks the question, "How much is the homeowner drawing from their home equity now or in the future?" The reason this is important is because they are not required to borrow much right now. Some lenders require a minimum loan balance of $50 or $100 to keep the account active. But the borrower may want to access significant funds at a later date when the line of credit has grown substantially. So, are the annual costs of this loan expensive? 6% interest on a balance of $100 equals $6 annually. So, this would be a very **INEXPENSIVE** mortgage when counting dollar costs.

Chapter 16

What do HECMs COST?

Unlike the previous question, answering this one is relatively easy. The costs are clearly itemized, and lenders are required to provide a Good Faith Estimate (GFE) of the charges at application. However, we can break the costs into up-front costs and ongoing costs.

UP-FRONT COSTS

Every loan is unique, but there are generally four types of up-front costs.

1. **Out of Pocket Costs:** Generally Appraisal Fees and Counseling Fees

2. **Origination Fees:** This cannot exceed 2% of the first $200,000 in home value and 1% of the home value that exceeds $200,000, with a hard cap of $6,000. The one exception is that HUD allows a minimum of $2,500.

3. **Initial Mortgage Insurance Premiums:** This charge will either be 0.5% or 2.5% of the maximum claim amount, depending on the amount of principal limit the homeowner intends to use during the initial disbursement period.

4. **Closing Costs and Third-Party Fees:** This may include Settlement Fees, Title Insurance, Attorney Fees, Recording Fees, etc.

Some of these costs may be off-set by some lender credits or broker credits for which the homeowner may be eligible. Also, HECM costs are generally financed into the loan so the borrower does not have to pay out-of-pocket. But these are costs nonetheless.

Let's look at an EXAMPLE

If Karen needs to access a large portion of her principal limit within the first year, she will pay 2.5% of her home value upfront as initial mortgage insurance premium (IMIP). She could have costs of up to 2% in origination fees, and possibly 1.5% or more in third-party closing costs. That could be **6%** of the home value at the time of closing.

Alternatively, if Karen needs to access a very small portion of her principal limit within the first year, she would pay 0.5% of her home value upfront as initial mortgage insurance premium (IMIP). Depending on the rate selected and market conditions, Karen may be offered lender credits. This may offset many of the other costs. In this case, Karen's net upfront costs could be less than **1%** of the home value at the time of closing.

ONGOING COSTS

The ongoing costs of the loan depend on many factors including: how the program is used, how much is drawn, when the funds are drawn, how much the home appreciates, and when the homeowner vacates the home.

This is a loan after all. Therefore, the amount that is borrowed will accrue interest and mortgage insurance. This will cause the loan balance to rise. Imagine, however, a homeowner that only carries a $100 balance, using the line of credit and its growth as an emergency fund. With a 4.75% interest rate and 1.25% in annual mortgage insurance, the reoccurring cost to this borrower could be as little as $6.00 per year.

Let's look at REFERENCES

Section 255 of the National Housing Act (12 U.S.C. 1715z–20)
LIMITATION ON ORIGINATION FEES

The Secretary shall establish limits on the origination fee that may be charged to a mortgagor under a mortgage insured under this section, which limitations shall:

(1) be equal to 2.0 percent of the maximum claim amount of the mortgage, up to a maximum claim amount of $200,000 plus 1 percent of any portion of the maximum claim amount that is greater than $200,000;

(2) be subject to a minimum allowable amount;

(3) provide that the origination fee may be fully financed with the mortgage;

(4) include any fees paid to correspondent mortgagees approved by the Secretary;

(5) have the same effective date as subsection (m)(2) regarding the limitation on principal obligation; and

(6) be subject to a maximum origination fee of $6,000, except that such maximum limit shall be adjusted in accordance with the annual percentage increase in the Consumer Price Index of the Bureau of Labor Statistics of the Department of Labor in increments of $500 only when the percentage increase in such index, when applied to the maximum origination fee, produces dollar increases that exceed $500.

Chapter 17

Will this AFFECT MY TAXES or GOVERNMENT BENEFITS?

This is a major concern that comes up frequently in training conversations. Keep in mind, I am not a tax planner or financial planner, and rules regarding these items are subject to change. I can give some general guidelines, but we will want to handle these as separate issues here.

WILL IT AFFECT MY TAXES?

It depends. Funds received through a HECM are NOT considered income, and are therefore NOT taxable as such. However, if funds are drawn and placed into a bank account, they become an asset where interest can be earned. Any interest received from a new, or higher, bank account may be taxable.

On the flip side, there may be cases where accrued interest that is paid on a HECM balance may be deductible just like it is with traditional, forward, mortgages. Fees paid at closing and payments made toward a Reverse Mortgage balance may impact tax deductions. HECMs, however, do not require payments. So, interest will accrue, but is not "paid." There are no deductions that I am aware of unless a borrower actually makes payments that are applied to the item that is considered a deduction.

WILL IT AFFECT MY GOVERNMENT BENEFITS?

Again, it depends. Accessing a large sum of cash from home equity and placing it in a bank account might be a problem for certain benefits that are "means-tested." A "means test" is a way of determining whether someone is eligible for assistance. If an individual has the "means" to do without the assistance, they may not be eligible to receive it.

So, it depends on the answers to two questions:

1. **Is the government benefit affected by means testing?**
2. **Is the amount drawn on a monthly basis in excess of the benefit's limits?**

Social Security is not currently means tested, and only one portion of Medicare is means tested. Therefore, Social Security and Medicare are generally not affected by Reverse Mortgage proceeds. However, Supplemental Security (SSI) and Medicaid may have income or asset requirements. It will be important to know what amount held in a bank account could prevent one from receiving that assistance.

It is always a best practice for the homeowner to consult with a benefit administrator or advisor to make sure they are not jeopardizing their financial plan.

Let's look at REFERENCES

Federal Trade Commission: www.consumer.ftc.gov
Reverse mortgage loan advances are not taxable, and generally don't affect your Social Security or Medicare benefits. You retain the title to your home, and you don't have to make monthly repayments. The loan must be repaid when the last surviving borrower dies, sells the home, or no longer lives in the home as a principal residence.

Chapter 18

Why do I have to attend COUNSELING?

The U.S. Department of Housing and Urban Development wants an independent third party involved in the process to make sure the Reverse Mortgage is a good fit and will benefit the homeowners. They feel so strongly about this that large amounts of grant money is dedicated each year solely for this purpose.

Why do homeowners have to complete counseling? In short, because the regulators want to protect them. HUD doesn't want to endorse a financial tool that doesn't offer the homeowners a bona fide advantage. Therefore, all borrowers, co-borrowers, and non-borrowing spouses have to go through counseling. In fact, guardians, conservators, and "Power of Attorneys" (POAs) involved in the transaction are required to attend the counseling as well. Heirs are simply encouraged to attend, but it is not required.

Do I complete counseling over the phone or in-person?
For most homeowners, that is entirely up to them. However, certain states may have something to say about it. North Carolina, for one, requires all HECM counseling to be performed face to face. That can get a little tricky for an older adult with difficulties moving, much less driving. However, a few local agencies may be willing to come to the homeowner.

Who do I call?

You can search online for a HECM counselor at:

https://entp.hud.gov/idapp/html/hecm_agency_look.cfm

A Reverse Mortgage professional should have a list of approved counseling agencies prepared. Otherwise, you can call toll free 1 (800) 569-4287.

Can you recommend specific counselors?

No. Loan originators are not allowed to steer potential borrowers to particular counselors. On the flip side, counselors are also not allowed to steer potential borrowers to particular lenders, mortgage brokers, or mortgage bankers.

BENEFITS CHECK-UP

This is a non-profit service from the National Council on Aging (NCOA) that is designed to identify ways that older adults can save money and cover daily expenses. During HECM counseling, the counselor may ask questions with the intention of finding federal and state resources that can improve the homeowner's ability to stay at home and meet their financial obligations.

THE PROCESS

This is my recommended process:

1. **Initial Discussion:** Review the HECM product with an experienced Reverse Mortgage Professional (RMP). Many forward mortgage professional are not aware of the intricacies involved in originating HECMs.

2. **Pre-Counseling Package:** Obtain this from the RMP. It should include the following documentation:

   - A counseling list that includes numbers for national and local agencies
   - "Preparing for Your Counseling Session" document

- A Loan Comparison of various product options
- A Total Annual Loan Cost (TALC) rate disclosure
- An Amortization Schedule
- "Use Your Home to Stay at Home" booklet from NCOA

3. **Complete Counseling:** Complete a counseling session with a HUD-approved counselor, with all required parties involved. The counselor will send certificates which must be signed and dated by all parties. The lender is restricted in what they can do until a fully signed and dated counseling certificate is provided.

4. **Complete a Loan Application:** Contact your chosen Reverse Mortgage Professional to complete the application, which is also called a "Form 1009."

Let's look at REFERENCES

HUD Handbook 4235.1 Chapter 1-9. COUNSELING

The borrower is required to receive counseling before the HECM application is processed. Counseling will be provided by HUD-approved housing counseling agencies and will focus on the different types of home equity conversion mortgages available, the suitability of a home equity conversion mortgage for the borrower, and the alternatives to a home equity conversion mortgage.

Mortgagee Letter 2011-26 HECM COUNSELOR LIST

ML 2010-37 requires lenders to provide each client with a list of HECM counseling agencies. Effective with this mortgagee letter, the national and regional intermediaries that must always be included on the list provided to borrowers will include those Intermediaries awarded HECM counseling grant funds by HUD.

(continued)

HUD Handbook 4235.1 Chapter 2-3.
COUNSELING REFERRAL PROCEDURES

The procedures below should be followed to ensure that the borrower receives the required counseling at the time he or she applies for a HECM. If the lender receives a request from a borrower to apply for a HECM, the lender should refer the borrower to a housing counseling agency for counseling by providing the borrower with a list of the names, addresses and phone numbers of the HUD-approved counseling agencies in the area. At the time that the lender refers the borrower to a counseling agency, it may provide the borrower with copies of the mortgage, note and Loan Agreement. The lender may complete the borrower's application before referral, however, the lender cannot charge the borrower for this service if the borrower does not choose to attend a counseling session or apply for a HECM after counseling. The lender cannot begin the process of ordering a property appraisal or any other action that would result in a charge to the potential borrower until the borrower has received counseling, and the lender has received the counseling certificate from the borrower.

24 CFR § 206.41. COUNSELING

List provided. At the time of the initial contact with the prospective mortgagor, the mortgagee shall give the mortgagor a list of the names, addresses, and telephone numbers of housing counselors and their employing agencies, which have been approved by the Secretary.

Chapter 19

What are my OBLIGATIONS
as the homeowner?

Monthly principal and interest payments are NOT ongoing obligations for the homeowner. But failure to keep up with other required homeowner obligations could cause a homeowner to be in DEFAULT on the mortgage and even cause a FORECLOSURE. Let's review the obligations that must be upheld.

OCCUPY THE HOME

Federal regulations require that a HECM borrower occupy the subject property as their "principal residence." In addition, the lender or servicer is required to document this with an occupancy certificate. If the home is not occupied because it is being purchased using the HECM for Purchase option, the borrower has 60 days from closing in which to move into the home.

PAY ALL PROPERTY CHARGES

This is one of the most important messages every homeowner needs to hear. It is imperative that they always pay their property charges. This could include:

• Property Taxes
• Homeowners Insurance Premiums
• Condo Association Dues
• Home Owner Association (HOA) Dues
• Any other property charges that are required to be paid.

Not doing so could jeopardize the homeowner's ability to stay in the home, whether they have a Reverse Mortgage or not. While the HECM does not require monthly principal and interest payments, HUD DOES require that property charges are paid, or foreclosure could result.

UPKEEP THE HOME

This may be a little subjective, but federal regulations state the home must be kept "IN GOOD REPAIR." FHA, as the insurer is very concerned about the value of the home. So, failure to maintain it can be considered a violation of the loan agreement.

Let's look at REFERENCES
24 CFR § 206.27. MORTGAGE PROVISIONS
The mortgagor shall maintain hazard insurance on the property in an amount acceptable to the Secretary and the mortgagee.

The mortgagor shall not participate in a real estate tax deferral program or permit any liens to be recorded against the property, unless such liens are subordinate to the insured mortgage and any second mortgage held by the Secretary.

A mortgage may be prepaid in full or in part in accordance with § 206.209.

The mortgagor must keep the property in good repair.

The mortgagor must pay taxes, hazard insurance premiums, ground rents and assessments in a timely manner, except to the extent such property charges are paid by the mortgagee in accordance with § 206.205.

The mortgagor shall be charged for the payment of monthly MIP.

Chapter 20

Why do I have to pay
MORTGAGE INSURANCE?

HECM loans are insured by the Federal Housing Administration (FHA), and therefore mortgage insurance premium (MIP) is required to be added to the loan. In most cases, the borrower will roll these costs into the loan balance, and the servicer will pay these as needed on their behalf. These funds end up in a pool of money called the Mutual Mortgage Insurance Fund (MMIF). FHA will use these funds to pay out insurance claims resulting from the non-recourse feature.

However, most homeowners and heirs are unaware that this insurance is for their advantage. This is how FHA can guarantee the non-recourse feature; the homeowner will not owe more than the home is worth at the time it is sold.

FHA offers this insurance with no profit margin designed to benefit the federal government. In fact, the changes to the program announced on Sept. 3, 2013, were implemented to eliminate some of the losses the HECM program has experienced over the last few years.

The MIP is what allows the HECM program to exist. Private lenders do not offer non-recourse mortgage programs at attractive rates. When the lender carries a risk of a home becoming upside-down, they will generally charge higher rates and reduce the principal limits.

There are two types of insurance premiums that are charged on each loan: IMIP and Annual MIP.

INITIAL MIP (IMIP)

This is a fee added to the closing costs, and is either going to be 2.50% or 0.50% of the maximum claim amount, depending on the amount the homeowner needs to borrow during the initial disbursement period. The amount of principal limit intended to be borrowed is sometimes referred to as "principal limit usage" or PLU.

2.50% of the MCA — For High PLU loans
0.50% of the MCA — For Low PLU loans

So, the question becomes "How LOW does my borrowed amount need to be in order to reduce my premium to 0.50%?" FHA set the threshold at 60% of the borrower's principal limit. Homeowners that need to access more than 60% of their principal limit will be charged the higher IMIP rate.

Let's look at an EXAMPLE

Charles has a home valued at $400,000. Based on his age and interest rate, his principal limit is $200,000. 60% of his principal limit would be $120,000.

If Charles needs to access more than $120,000 to pay off his existing mortgage liens plus closing costs, he will have an IMIP cost at closing of 2.50% of $400,000, or **$10,000**.

If Charles needs to access $120,000 or less to pay off his existing mortgage liens plus closing costs, he will have an IMIP cost at closing of 0.50% of $400,000, or **$2,000**.

ANNUAL MIP (MIP)

The annual charges are quite different. This is calculated at an annual rate of 1.25% of the unpaid principal balance (Loan Balance). Even though this is an annual rate, it is processed monthly at a rate of 1/12th of 1.25%, or 0.104%.

Let's look at REFERENCES

HUD 4235.1 Chapter 1-10 MORTGAGE INSURANCE

The borrower will be charged mortgage insurance premiums to reduce the risk of loss in the event that the outstanding balance, including accrued interest, MIP, and fees, exceeds the value of the property at the time that the mortgage is due and payable.

Mortgagee Letter 2013-27. INITIAL MIP

HUD will charge an initial MIP of 0.50 percent (0.50%) of the Maximum Claim Amount (MCA) when the sum of the mortgagor's initial disbursement at closing and other required or available disbursements during the First 12-Month Disbursement Period is 60% or less of the Principal Limit. HUD will charge an initial MIP of 2.50 percent (2.50%) of the MCA when a mortgagor's initial disbursement at closing and other required or available disbursements during the First 12-Month Disbursement Period are greater than 60% of the available Principal Limit.

Chapter 21

What if my SPOUSE
IS NOT 62 or older?

When a spouse is NOT included in a HECM transaction, he/she is referred to as a Non-Borrowing Spouse (NBS). This is often due to the spouse not meeting the age requirement (age 62). In a simple sense, an NBS is the spouse of a Reverse Mortgage borrower who will NOT be on the Reverse Mortgage, and will NOT be on title to the home.

THE PROBLEM

As noted above, some spouses are not included in Reverse Mortgages because they are not old enough. However, there are other reasons. For example, homeowners who have pre-nup agreements, homeowners who have been remarried and want biological children to inherit their estates, or homeowners who don't intend to stay married, may all choose to leave their spouses off the loans.

Nevertheless, these NBSs have historically NOT been protected after the deaths of their spouses. If the last borrower died, the loan became "due and payable"...even though the surviving spouse was still living in the home. While this was not good public relations for Reverse Mortgages, the surviving spouses never actually "owned" the homes. As a result, a non-borrowing spouse who remained would have to probate the will, and then sell the home or attempt to refinance the home in his/her own name.

THE SOLUTION

As a result of AARP's involvement on behalf of surviving spouses, HUD has determined that an NBS should have additional rights as a "homeowner." They felt the loan should NOT be due and payable until a surviving NBS dies or moves out of the home. This is called a "Deferral Period", and became eligible for loans with FHA Case numbers assigned Aug. 4, 2014, and later.

On that same day, new principal limit factor (PLF) tables were issued to accommodate non-borrowing spouses. In essence, HUD now will allow a deferral period for an NBS, but has reduced the principal limits for borrowers married to them.

Non-Borrowing Spouse PLFs

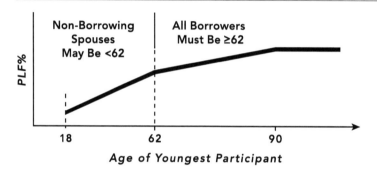

As the diagram shows, borrowers will still need to be at least 62 years old. Older borrowers (up to age 90) generally have larger PLFs, while borrowers married to someone under 62, will have reduced principal limits. As noted earlier, PLFs are now based on the age of the youngest borrower, co-borrower, or non-borrowing spouse.

But the guidelines for NBSs are actually not that simple, and are commonly misunderstood. So, let's see if I can explain in greater detail. FHA changed the guidelines in 2014 so that spouses may continue living in their homes following the death of the last borrower.

However, this created another issue: Having an NBS generally meant the borrower would have access to less funds. This was because the borrower's available funds became based on the NBS's age. This was true whether the NBS was qualified for the deferment or not.

THE CLARIFICATION

Some lenders argued that if an NBS is not "qualified", they shouldn't be required to use the age of that NBS in the calculation of the borrower's Principal Limit. As a result, FHA modified guidelines in 2015 to create new designations—Ineligible and Eligible Non-Borrowing Spouses.

An INELIGIBLE Non-Borrowing Spouse:
• Generally does not occupy the home;

• Is not protected by the NBS "due and payable" deferral provisions; and

• Does not have their age included in the calculation of the borrower's principal limit

An ELIGIBLE Non-Borrowing Spouse:
• Occupies the home

• Is protected by the NBS "due and payable" deferral provisions, and

• Has his/her age included in the calculation of the borrower's principal limit

QUALIFYING FOR THE DEFERRAL PERIOD

After the death of the last borrower, the due and payable status of the mortgage may be deferred for an Eligible NBS. However, in order to be eligible for the deferral, the NBS must:

• Have been the borrower's spouse at the time of closing;

• Have remained the borrower's spouse during the time the HECM was in service;

• Have been disclosed to the lender at origination;

• Have been named as an NBS in the loan documents; and must

• Continue to occupy the home as their Principal Residence

In addition, if the last borrower has passed on, it will be imperative that the NBS establish legal ownership of the home within 90 days. At that point, the NBS will need to make sure to keep up with any obligations of the HECM, including payment of property charges, to ensure the loan does not become due and payable for other reasons.

Because an NBS has only limited protection as a homeowner, and no access to the available line-of-credit following the death of the borrower, we would prefer to have both parties involved. We would prefer NOT to have an NBS. However, if a spouse is under 62, the only other option is to wait.

Let's look at REFERENCES

Mortgagee Letter 2014-07. NON -BORROWING SPOUSE

For any HECM with a case number issued after the effective date of this Mortgagee Letter, in order to be eligible for FHA insurance, the HECM must contain a provision deferring the due and payable status that occurs because of the death of the last surviving mortgagor, if a mortgagor was married at the time of closing and the Non-Borrowing Spouse was identified at the time of closing. Specifically, the HECM documents must contain a provision deferring due and payable status until the death of the last surviving Non-Borrowing Spouse or until another listed event occurs.

Mortgagee Letter 2015-02. ELIGIBLE AND INELIGIBLE NON-BORROWING HECM SPOUSES

At application, the mortgagee must identify any current Non-Borrowing Spouse and must determine if the Non-Borrowing Spouse is currently eligible or ineligible for a Deferral Period. This determination is a factual determination and cannot be changed or waived by any election. A Non-Borrowing Spouse that meets the Qualifying Attributes requirements at applica-tion for a Deferral Period is an Eligible Non-Borrowing Spouse and may not elect to be ineligible. Similarly, a Non-Borrowing Spouse that is ineligible at application because he or she does not satisfy the Qualifying Attributes requirements for a Deferral Period may not elect to be eligible.

Chapter 22

What do I need to know about INTEREST RATES?

There are multiple rates one might encounter though the Reverse Mortgage process. I have taught many classes on HECM math, and it is my favorite topic. But because this is a bigger topic, it might help if I break it down into multiple smaller discussions on rates.

FIXED vs. ADJUSTABLE RATES

By now you already know that HECMs can be fixed as well as adjustable. The **HECM-FIXED** has rates that never change over the life of the loan. The currently offered **HECM-ARMs** are tied to either the 1-month LIBOR index or the 1-year LIBOR Index.

PRODUCT	WHEN WILL THE RATE CHANGE?
HECM-Fixed	The rate will NOT change over the life of the loan
Monthly HECM-ARM	The rate may change (adjust) monthly
Annual HECM-ARM	The rate may change (adjust) annually

THE LIBOR INDEX

The London Inter-Bank Offered Rate is an INDEX that, when added to the lender margin, produces the current interest rate on the adjustable rate HECM. When this goes up, a borrower's interest rate goes up.

Lender Margin	+	LIBOR Index	=	Interest Rate
2.750%	+	1.500%	=	4.250%

The LIBOR Index is not something that can be locked. It will simply move up or down and affect the amount of interest that accrues on the loan.

LENDER MARGIN

The lender has expectations about what interest they wish to receive on an ARM loan above the current index rate. So, this margin is added to the ARM's index as we discussed in the previous section. Generally, lower margins are preferred by most borrowers. Larger margins put the borrower at a higher loan compounding rate, but they also improve the homeowner's line of credit growth.

EXPECTED RATES

With fixed rate loans, FHA knows what each loan's rate will be in the future. If it was 4.99% at the start, it will still be 4.99% in ten years. The HECM-ARM rates, however, are not known because they can change every month or every year. Therefore, FHA uses a market indicator called the 10-year SWAP to predict what the LIBOR Index will be in the future. When the SWAP is added to the lender margin, the result is the **expected rate** (ER) or **expected interest rate** of the loan.

Lender Margin	+	10-Yr SWAP	=	Expected Interest Rate
2.750%	+	2.500%	=	5.250%

INTEREST RATE CAPS

Interest Rate Caps are there to protect the homeowner if interest rates rise dramatically. On forward mortgages, ARM loans without caps can be dangerous because the monthly payment can fluctuate up or down with interest rates. That is NOT true with Reverse Mortgages, as they do not require monthly principal and interest payments. The caps on the HECM-ARM, however, are there to protect the homeowner from excessive compounding of the loan balance.

The Monthly LIBOR HECM-ARM Cap has historically been 10% above the start rate. This means a loan that begins at 4.5% will never have an interest rate that exceeds 14.5%. This is called a "lifetime cap." Some lenders may offer this product with caps as low as 5%.

The Annual LIBOR HECM-ARM has historically offered 2% caps per adjustment and 5% caps over the lifetime. This means the rate cannot rise or fall by more than 2% each year, and will not rise or fall more than 5% over the life of the loan.

Let's look at REFERENCES ────────────

Mortgagee Letter 2007-13. THE LIBOR INDEX

In addition, this final rule amended HUD's regulation at 24 CFR 206.3 to add the use of both the 1-Month LIBOR index and the 1-Month Constant Maturity Treasury (CMT) index for calculating the interest rate adjustments on the monthly adjusting Home Equity Conversion Mortgage (HECM). The final rule also permits the 1-Year LIBOR index for calculating the interest rate adjustments on the annually adjusting HECM. The 10-Year LIBOR swap rate shall be used to calculate the Expected Interest Rate on LIBOR-indexed HECMs.

(continued)

24 CFR 206.3 EXPECTED RATES

Expected average mortgage interest rate means the interest rate used to calculate the principal limit and the future payments to the mortgagor and is established based on the date on which the initial loan application is signed by the borrower.

For adjustable rate HECMs, it is…the sum of the mortgagee's margin plus the 10-year LIBOR swap rate.

Chapter 23

What can you tell me about the LOC FEATURES?

Quite possibly the most amazing feature of the adjustable rate HECM product is the line of credit (LOC) and its ability to grow. It is only available on the adjustable rate products, and it is unique in the world of finance. It is also the primary reason Reverse Mortgages are useful in financial planning. However, let's list and discuss six primary advantages of having a line of credit.

1. Funds left in the LOC do not hurt the homeowner.

By hurt, I mean accrue interest or mortgage insurance. These are the customary charges that would cause one's loan balance to rise. But the homeowner will only accrue charges on their loan balance.

2. It is "OPEN-ENDED" credit.

This means one can borrow from it, pay it down, and borrow from it again without restriction. In fact, many will use the LOC as a form of cash flow management for business or personal use.

3. It is "LIQUID" home equity.

Liquid means "easily converted to cash". The funds that are requested from a HECM servicer (in writing) are required to be wired to the borrower's bank account within 5 business days. Generally, home equity cannot be accessed so quickly. One would either need to sell the home, refinance, or obtain a home equity line of credit using traditional means to access those funds. Those methods not only take time, but come with their own upfront and/or monthly costs.

4. It is considered "PLEDGED FUNDS".

The LOC is not classified as an asset. These funds are "pledged" to the borrower(s). This means that the growth is not taxable. This also means that the LOC itself cannot be willed or given away. These are simply funds that are pledged to the borrower if they ever need them. If the borrower ever DOES need them, the desired funds may be drawn, and those funds would then become an asset to them.

5. It is "SECURE".

The LOC is not capped, reduced, frozen or eliminated as a result of market conditions or property value declines. I personally had a traditional home equity line of credit (HELOC) that was eliminated in 2008, when my property value declined. But the HECM does not operate that way, which is another reason it can be trusted for financial planning.

6. It GROWS!

Lastly, the most compelling feature is the ability for the available LOC to grow, which we will explore next.

Let's look at REFERENCES ─────────────
HUD 4235.1 Chapter 1-5C LINE OF CREDIT
Under this payment plan, the borrower will receive the mortgage proceeds in unscheduled payments or in installments, at times and in amounts of the borrower's choosing, until the line of credit is exhausted.

HUD 4235.1 Chapter 5-3C LINE OF CREDIT
The borrower may elect to make withdrawals at times and in amounts of his or her choosing, as long as he or she maintains the property as a principal residence.

HUD 4235.1 Chapter 5-7A
DETERMINING THE NET PRINCIPAL LIMIT
To determine the maximum amount of payments that a borrower can receive after closing, the net principal limit is calculated.

The net principal limit is calculated by subtracting from the principal limit any initial payments to or on behalf of the borrower, such as the initial MIP, closing costs, or cash payment to the borrower, and any funds set aside from the principal limit for monthly servicing fees or set asides for repairs after closing and first-year property charges. The net principal limit may be drawn by a borrower as monthly payments, or as a line of credit, or both.

HUD 4235.1 Chapter 5-9 NET PRINCIPAL LIMIT
A line of credit is limited by the net principal limit for every month that the mortgage is outstanding.

The borrower can withdraw the entire net principal limit on the first day of a mortgage...The borrower could still live in the house as long as he or she chose.

If the maximum amount is not withdrawn at closing, a borrower can make withdrawals at times and in amounts of his or her choosing as long as the withdrawal does not cause the outstanding balance to exceed the principal limit for the month in which the withdrawal is made. The available line of credit is the net principal limit for the month in which the withdrawal is made.

Chapter 24

What can you tell me
about LOC GROWTH?

Once again, this is a compelling argument for why nearly every qualified homeowner should get a Reverse Mortgage. The LOC growth means these pledged funds will not only be liquid and secure, they may also grow to be much larger.

There are 2 factors that cause LOCs to grow:

1. <u>**LOC growth rate:**</u> This causes the LOC to grow organically at a rate equal to the compounding rate. This rate can be described as [Interest Rate + 1.25%].

2. <u>**Making payments:**</u> Any payments made to reduce the unpaid principal balance will also cause the line of credit to rise. Most loan originators are unaware that the LOC is boosted with each payment.

The lesson to be learned by this is that if a borrower has cash available, it would be prudent to use it to pay down the Reverse Mortgage balance, thereby boosting the LOC by that amount. The increased LOC will then continue to grow at the compounding rate, available for future use.

Let's look at an EXAMPLE

Stephen has a Reverse Mortgage loan balance of $70,000 and a line of credit valued at $45,000. He sells a car valued at $10,000, and intends to keep the cash available for any contingencies. If Stephen were to use the funds to reduce his loan balance to $60,000, it would not only reduce his interest charges, but it would also boost his growing LOC to $55,000.

IT CAN EXCEED THE HOME'S VALUE

In cases where borrower(s) hold a growing LOC for longer periods, or where interest rates rise dramatically causing the LOC to grow faster, or if property values decline, then the LOC may exceed the home's value. This is acceptable, and borrowers are permitted to draw funds that exceed their home's value.

LOC Growth

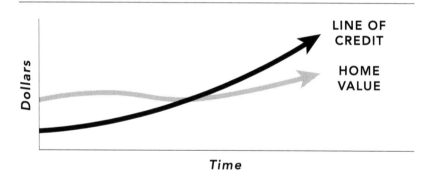

IT IS GUARANTEED TO GROW

If a loan has a lender margin of 2.75%, and the LIBOR Index is 2.00%, then the sum of these two plus 1.25% would give the loan an LOC growth rate of 6%. In this example, even if the LIBOR Index were to drop to 0%, the LOC would be growing at 4%.

PRECAUTIONS

This LOC is ONLY available on the adjustable rate products. Fixed rate loans are closed end, meaning NO LOC is established, and paying down the balance does not give a borrower the right to draw it back again.

Also, it is important to know that ONLY the AVAILABLE LOC grows. Some borrowers use all of their LOC funds and wonder why their LOC does not increase the next month. There is simply nothing to increase.

Let's look at REFERENCES
24 CFR § 206.25. CALCULATION OF PAYMENTS
Line of credit separately or with monthly payments. If the mortgagor has a line of credit...the line of credit amount increases at the same rate as the total principal limit increases under § 206.3. A payment under the line of credit may not exceed the difference between the current amount of the principal limit for the line of credit and the portion of the mortgage balance, including accrued interest and MIP, attributable to draws on the line of credit.

HUD Handbook 4235.1 Chapter 5-12.
PARTIAL PREPAYMENTS
A borrower may prepay all or part of the outstanding balance at any time without penalty. However, no prepayment of an amount in excess of the outstanding balance is allowed.

A borrower may choose to make a partial prepayment to set up or to increase a line of credit without altering existing monthly payments. By reducing the outstanding balance, the borrower increases the net principal limit. All or part of the increase in the net principal limit may be set aside for a line of credit.

Chapter 25

What is HECM FOR PURCHASE?

This variation to the HECM program is no longer "new." Unfortunately, older homeowners are still not aware of the advantages. HECM for Purchase began with the passage of the Housing and Economic Recovery Act of 2008. Prior to this legislation, if a homeowner in retirement wanted to relocate, qualifying for the new home often proved difficult. They would have to be eligible to purchase a home though traditional means, establish their residency in the home, and then refinance with a HECM if desired as shown in the diagram below:

PRE-2008

| Purchase a Home (CLOSING) | Establish Residency (WAIT) | Refinance to a HECM (CLOSING) |

As you can see, this included two sets of closing costs for the new home, and a waiting period called "seasoning" that could have been as long as a year. It was expensive and time-consuming.

POST-2008

Purchase a Home using a HECM
(One closing, and no waiting period)

Now, homeowners can more easily relocate to be closer to family, downsize to a more manageable home/townhouse/condo, or even upsize to a retirement dream home on the beach, golf course, or active adult community.

In a HECM for Purchase, the lender will still be able to provide the same principal limit to the borrower. However, instead of giving the funds to the borrower, the funds are generally applied to the sales price of the new home.

Let's look at an EXAMPLE

Based on Pamela's age and expected interest rate, she qualifies for a principal limit factor of 60%. Remember, this is a percentage of the home's value that the lender can offer the borrower. Pamela is moving to be closer to family, and has just sold a home—netting $200,000 in gain on the sale. This leaves her with significantly more cash than is needed to purchase the new home using a HECM.

New home sales price	$300,000
Lender contributes 60%	$180,000
Pamela comes to closing with	$120,000 + closing costs

She can pocket the remaining $80,000 she didn't need, and add this to her retirement savings.

While $120,000 seems like a significant down payment, borrowers like Pamela are selling their existing residences. The following diagram is a graphical illustration of how Pamela upsized to a larger home:

HECM for Purchase: Upsize

CURRENT HOME

$200K

$200K
Gain on Sale

NEW HOME

$300K

$180K from **HECM**
$120K from **Funds from Sale**
($80K Cash Remaining)

While it is not uncommon to see the HECM for Purchase used in this manner to UPSIZE to a larger dream home, it is more likely that the homeowner will be selling their current home to relocate or DOWNSIZE to something more manageable.

HECM for Purchase: Downsize

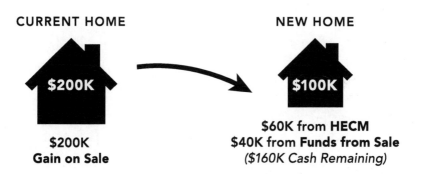

CURRENT HOME

$200K

$200K
Gain on Sale

NEW HOME

$100K

$60K from **HECM**
$40K from **Funds from Sale**
($160K Cash Remaining)

In this case, downsizing using a HECM for Purchase leaves Pamela with significant funds left over ($160,000) with which she can supplement her retirement savings.

THE DETAILS

Occupancy:

HECMs are specifically designed to be offered only for a borrower's "Principal Residence." This means that HUD will require the borrower to occupy the home within 60 days.

New Construction:

Be careful if the home to be purchased is considered "New Construction." HUD guidelines state that the home must be 100% complete and the Certificate of Occupancy or its equivalent must be issued prior to the initial application.

Lender Overlays:

Each lender has program guidelines that may be added to the HUD guidelines. These are called "OVERLAYS," and for the HECM for Purchase, one might find restrictions that will make qualifying for the HECM for Purchase more difficult.

Sales Contract:

The lender will require the sales contract to be fully-executed (signed) before an application is taken. They also require either an original copy of the sales contract, or one that has every page stamped "true and certified." Make sure all exhibits are included.

Seller Paid Closing Costs:

This is an area where many mistakes are made. HUD is very restrictive regarding any type of seller concessions.

This program option is a little tricky, only because it is so seldom used. So maybe this step-by-step process for the perfect HECM for Purchase will help:

1. **Obtain HECM Counseling:** The Counseling Certificate should reflect the borrower's current address, not the home that is being considered, as that may change before closing.

2. **Determine whether the applicant wishes to retain their existing home:** If the answer is "yes," know that the borrower will need to "income qualify" to show that they have sufficient funds to pay the existing home's property charges as well as the new home's property charges.

3. **New Construction:** Confirm that the home has a certificate of occupancy or an equivalent designation.

4. **Negotiate the Sales Contract:** Ensure that it does not include any seller concessions. FHA is very restrictive with regard to fees paid by the seller at closing.

5. **Sign the Sales Contract:** Retain a copy with the FHA amendatory clause and all exhibits for the loan officer.

6. **Apply for the HECM for Purchase:** Know that this can take some time to process and underwrite.

7. **Attend Closing:** Make sure to establish occupancy of the Home within 60 days.

Let's look at REFERENCES

Mortgagee Letter 2008-33. HECM FOR PURCHASE

The Housing and Economic Recovery Act of 2008 (HERA) provides HECM mortgagors with the opportunity to purchase a new principal residence with HECM loan proceeds. Section 2122(a)(9) of HERA amends section 255 of the National Housing Act to authorize the Department of Housing and Urban Development (HUD) to insure HECMs used for the purchase of a 1- to 4-family dwelling unit. Accordingly, eligible mortgagors now have the opportunity to purchase a principal residence with HECM loan proceeds. HECM for purchase transactions, for which the FHA case number is assigned on or after January 1, 2009, must satisfy existing program requirements and the provisions of this Mortgagee Letter.

Chapter 26

What if my home needs REPAIRS?

Renovating or repairing a home is a common reason one would consider a Reverse Mortgage. But there are three types of repairs:

- **Repairs that are required to be done prior to closing,**

- **Repairs where funds are set aside to be completed after closing, and**

- **Renovations**

PRIOR TO CLOSING

Typical repairs that must be completed before the loan can be cleared for closing would include structural defects and health or safety concerns. Structural defects could include foundation issues, electrical issues, and roof leaks. Health and safety concerns could include standing water, black mold, or even clutter that restricts proper navigation of the home.

REPAIR SET-ASIDES

For most other repairs, a portion of the principal limit may be set aside. These funds can be held for the payment of those repairs.

Even if the quote is $100 for a minor repair, the lender may still require a minimum set-aside amount plus an additional fee for re-inspection.

RENOVATIONS

When a homeowner decides that this is the home where they wish to stay, there are often renovations that will make their retiring years easier. These could include handrails in the bathrooms, a walk-in bathtub, and railings or ramps near outside steps.

What about a major overhaul or remodel of the home? HUD has set a limit of 15% of the maximum claim amount for large-scale renovations.

Let's look at an EXAMPLE

Cynthia's home is valued at $200,000. Unfortunately, the home needs a lot of work, and the costs are estimated at $45,000. HUD's repair limit for this property is calculated at 15% of $200,000, or $30,000. Cynthia will need to have $15,000 of the repairs completed prior to closing to meet the homes repair limit.

Let's look at REFERENCES

24 CFR § 206.47. PROPERTY STANDARDS; REPAIR WORK

Need for repairs. Properties must meet the applicable property standards of the Secretary in order to be eligible. Properties which do not meet the property standards must be repaired in order to ensure that the repaired property will serve as adequate security for the insured mortgage.

Assurance that repairs are made. The mortgage may be closed before the repair work is completed if the Secretary estimates that the cost of the remaining repair work will not exceed 15 percent of the maximum claim amount and the mortgage contains provisions approved by the Secretary concerning payment for the repairs.

Chapter 27

What happens
if I MAKE PAYMENTS toward
a HECM balance?

There are significant advantages in making payments toward HECM loan balances that are not well known. Many homeowners are too intrigued by the fact that HECMs don't REQUIRE a payment. Unfortunately, they miss a great opportunity to maximize some advantages of a HECM.

LOAN BALANCE REDUCTION

Of course, payments will tend to reduce the homeowner's loan balance. This advantage is no different than most other loans. If the borrower is capable of making payments, then reducing the loan balance on a Reverse Mortgage will reduce the interest and mortgage insurance accruals on the loan. This can protect the homeowner's equity as they will owe less on the mortgage.

A. Making Regular Payments *(Just Like Forward Mortgages)*

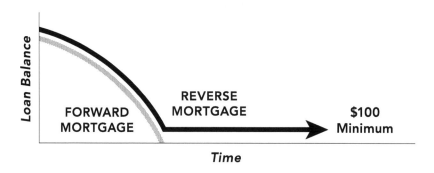

As this graph shows, the forward mortgage is paid off completely (loan balance = $0). If the same payments are consistently applied to the Reverse Mortgage, the reduction in loan balance should be very similar. The HECM loan balance, however, is paid down to a recommended $100 loan balance. This keeps the mortgage active and preserves the line of credit. **It is not advantageous to pay off the loan completely, as this would close the HECM.**

Many HECM borrowers will make periodic payments as certain investments mature or as they sell off other assets. This is advantageous as well.

B. Making Periodic Payments

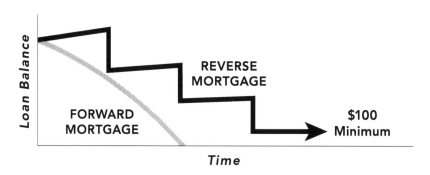

As the graph shows, interest and mortgage insurance accruals will cause the loan to rise. The payments, also known as "pre-payments" will knock the balance down. The loan balance will rise again until the next pre-payment is made.

BOOST YOUR LINE OF CREDIT

A second advantage of making payments toward an adjustable rate HECM loan balance is a potential boost in the line of credit (LOC). This opens up one of the hidden secrets of the HECM program. We already learned that the LOC will grow at the compounding rate (interest rate plus 1.25%), but the LOC ALSO grows when making payments. Many have argued that only that portion of the payment that is applied to principal will increase the borrower's LOC. They are mistaken. The available line of credit is calculated so that any reduction in loan balance will have a corresponding increase in LOC.

POSSIBLE TAX BENEFIT

For accounting and tax purposes, a portion of the payment may be allocated toward mortgage insurance and/or mortgage interest. This might have beneficial tax considerations, and the loan servicer will be required to issue a 1098 form in January, following a calendar year where payments were made.

Let's look at REFERENCES ────────────
24 CFR § 206.209. PREPAYMENT
No charge or penalty. The mortgagor may prepay a mortgage in full or in part without charge or penalty at any time, regardless of any limitations on prepayment stated in a mortgage.

HUD Handbook 4235.1 Chapter 5-12.
PARTIAL PREPAYMENTS
A borrower may prepay all or part of the outstanding balance at any time without penalty. However, no prepayment of an amount in excess of the outstanding balance is allowed.

A borrower may choose to make a partial prepayment because his or her financial circumstances have improved and he or she wishes to preserve more of the equity in the property. Any change in subsequent payments to the borrower should be made only at the borrower's request. Repayment in full will terminate the loan agreement.

A borrower may choose to use a partial prepayment to increase monthly payments. By reducing the outstanding balance, the borrower increases the net principal limit available for calculating monthly payments in accordance with Paragraph 5-8 of this chapter.

A borrower may choose to make a partial prepayment to set up or to increase a line of credit without altering existing monthly payments. By reducing the outstanding balance, the borrower increases the net principal limit. All or part of the increase in the net principal limit may be set aside for a line of credit.

Chapter 28

Isn't the Reverse Mortgage only for the DESPERATE?

No. But I can understand why many think this is true. There is a common misconception that the Reverse Mortgage is a "loan of last resort" for desperate homeowners facing foreclosure or bankruptcy. This stems from poor marketing that has given the public the wrong impression.

Yes, the Reverse Mortgage is a terrific life-saver program for those that are house rich, but cash poor, and NEED money right now. It CAN be viewed as an ATM machine for homeowners with significant equity but no cash. Unfortunately, many have taken this usage to its extreme and began to use this as a full-blown cash-out refinance. This is surely one of the many uses for HECMs. It can have a dramatic positive impact on a homeowner's quality of life, but it may not be the optimal strategy for many homeowners.

Let's look at the original intent of the Reverse Mortgage program. HUD's Handbook 4235 was designed to give us guidance on how the program should operate, and it starts with the purpose of the program; *"to enable elderly homeowners to convert the equity in their homes to monthly streams of income and/or lines of credit."*

Unfortunately, many brokers and lenders are not well equipped to explain or demonstrate the financial planning advantages this program has for those who are NOT desperate, or those who are independently wealthy. Many ideal candidates have no immediate need for government insured funds. But this program can be quite prudent for them as well, if used properly.

Let's look at an EXAMPLE

Patricia is 62 and has a home valued at $500,000. She has a retirement portfolio of $1 million and wants to retire. Patricia is surely not desperate or needy. She has, however, been advised that to make her retirement portfolio last, she needs to restrict her annual draws to no more than $50,000, which is not enough to pay her annual expenses. For her, the HECM can be used to add a stream of income that will allow Patricia to maintain her quality of life.

Being able to recognize the alternate uses of home equity in retirement requires one to take a long-term financial-planning view. Remember, the program was not initially designed as a short-term, quick fix. It was designed for two purposes:

1. **A monthly stream of income, or**
2. **A line of credit for future use**

Sure, a monthly income stream may ALSO be very useful for the desperate and needy. Our primary objective, however, as Reverse Mortgage Professionals is to make sure our clients have long-term strategies for occupying their homes with the ability to pay, not only their living expenses, but also any contingencies which may arise. The line of credit is discussed at length later in this book, and solves this problem. When viewed this way, the LOC can become a form of insurance. If, or when, the homeowner has desperate needs in the future, the LOC is available to assist, without disrupting the homeowner's retirement plan.

Let's look at REFERENCES
HUD Handbook 4235.1 Chapter 1-2.
PURPOSE OF THE PROGRAM.
The program insures what are commonly referred to as reverse mortgages, and is designed to enable elderly homeowners to convert the equity in their homes to monthly streams of income and/or lines of credit.

Chapter 29

What are the FINANCIAL PLANNING implications?

Financial planners, advisors, CPAs, estate planners, and other finance professionals are realizing that obtaining a Reverse Mortgage EARLY opens up potential income later in retirement. The basic premise is that the growing line of credit (LOC) is not taxed on its growth, and is a secure collection of funds that can act as **a second source of retirement reserves when needed.**

When a homeowner uses home equity as part of a comprehensive financial planning strategy, it is a form of diversification. For example, if the value of the home declines, an established LOC will continue to grow regardless. In this way, the HECM can act as form of **insurance against declining home values.**

In addition, the resulting larger LOC can be converted to monthly tenure or term payments at any time. As the LOC grows, and the homeowner gets older, converting the LOC to monthly tenure or term payments becomes more attractive. This is because larger dollar amounts will be distributed over shorter expected time periods. In this way, the HECM can act as form of **insurance against future cash flow issues later in life.**

THE HECM-ARM MAY BE MORE USEFUL THAN THE HECM-FIXED OPTION

The primary concept to understand about using the HECM as a tool for financial planning is that the fixed rate option is probably NOT the best option. There are three reasons why the adjustable rate HECM product might make more sense.

1. Future Draws

Fixed rate HECMs are currently "Single Disbursement Lump Sum Payment" loans. This means that the homeowner gets what they get at closing, and future draws are not available. Financial Planning, by its very definition, involves alternatives for the future, and the HECM-Fixed does not provide for that possibility.

2. Making Payments

When prepayments are made on the HECM-Fixed, it will reduce the unpaid principal balance. That's it. That's all it does. However, when prepayments are made on an adjustable rate HECM, it not only reduces the unpaid principal balance, but it also boosts the line of credit.

3. LOC Growth

The available line of credit grows because of two actions; PREPAYMENTS and the CREDIT LINE GROWTH RATE. This growth will be calculated at the interest rate plus 1.25%. This is at the heart of the Financial Planning advantage for an eligible senior.

Let's look at an EXAMPLE

Mark is 62 and owns his home worth $300,000. At age 62, with an expected rate of 5%, he could qualify for a principal limit of $157,200. After closing costs, a line of credit is established at approximately $150,000. He would only accrue interest and mortgage insurance premium (MIP) on the closing costs and funds that he needs from the LOC. Over the years, the LOC will continue to grow, and can exceed the home's value. This gives Mark the financial flexibility to handle unexpected financial pressures in his later years.

At some point during his retirement, Mark may want to convert his line of credit into a monthly term or tenure payment. Remember, he can do that at any time for a small $20 fee.

There are no pre-payment penalties on HECM loans, and as you can see, there are numerous advantages. For this reason, I would recommend that homeowners at least 62 years old, with forward loan balances, look into converting their forward mortgage into a Reverse Mortgage. Making the same payments on a HECM will still reduce the loan balance, but those payments will also open up future income opportunities.

Let's look at REFERENCES

HUD 4330.1 Chapter 13-21B.
ESTABLISH OR INCREASE A LINE OF CREDIT
A mortgagor may choose to make a partial prepayment to set up or to increase a line of credit without altering existing monthly payments. By reducing the outstanding balance, the mortgagor increases the net principal limit. All or part of the increase in the net principal limit may be set aside for a line of credit.

Chapter 30

Why not wait until I actually NEED a Reverse Mortgage?

When potential HECM borrowers delay getting Reverse Mortgages, there are three things that actually work in their favor. Therefore, one would assume that borrowers would normally get more funds by waiting, but that may not be the case.

THE BENEFITS OF WAITING

1. **The borrower is getting older.** This generally means higher PLFs later.

2. **The home generally appreciates.** This generally means higher principal limits later.

3. **The existing mortgage balance gets smaller.** This generally means higher net principal limits.

These three items indicate that it might make sense to wait. However, the following are two very powerful forces that may negate these three advantages.

THE COSTS OF WAITING

1. Expected interest rates (ER) are projected to be higher in the future.

2. The homeowner would have missed an opportunity for compounding LOC growth.

Remember, the 10-year SWAP Rate is one component of the expected rate. Higher SWAP rates translate into higher ERs, and small increases in ER can have a devastating impact on principal limit factors for new applicants.

Let's look at an EXAMPLE

Gary is 80 years old, and based on today's SWAP rates he has an expected interest rate of 5.25%. Referencing HUD's PLF Tables we can use this information to show Gary having a PLF of 62.7% today.

In five years, Gary will be 85 years old. Assuming HUD tables remain the same, this should give him higher PLFs of 67.1%. However, a rise in expected rates during those five years to 6.25% will drop his PLF to 57.0%.

As you can see, a 1% change in expected rates over five years can cause a dramatic reduction in PLF. When converted to dollars, Gary lost $5,700 in principal limit for every $100,000 in home value.

In addition, because the available line of credit grows over time, there is an opportunity cost of waiting that must be considered. This is not much different than the advice a financial planner would give to a 30-year-old; "why wait to start saving for retirement, the power of compounding growth is in your hands." The earliest a homeowner can qualify for a HECM and establish the LOC is at age 62.

The home may appreciate, and waiting will make the homeowner older. But obtaining a HECM now will allow the available line of credit to grow over a longer time period.

In addition, expected rates are not guaranteed to stay this low. While it is important not to rush into a decision to leverage your home equity for financial planning purposes, I would recommend considering it as early as possible for these reasons.

In fact, it can be argued that a 62 year old with a few years left to pay on a forward mortgage may be an ideal candidate for a Home Equity Conversion as of the writing of this book. This is because a 62 year old will have a longer life expectancy, allowing more LOC growth. During this time, the homeowner is paying down a loan balance. When interest rates rise, the LOC can rapidly grow while the mortgage loan balance remains at a low $100. Remember, HECM servicers may require a minimum loan balance in order for the HECM to remain open/active.

Chapter 31

How did recent CHANGES affect the program?

The short answer is DRAMATICALLY! The changes in 2013 were major, and were the most significant changes since the first HECM was originated in 1989. Fortunately, the changes of the last few years strengthened the HECM program and added more consumer protections. That is one of the primary reasons I felt this book was necessary.

2013 CHANGES

The most significant changes of 2013 were the introduction of initial disbursement limits, and initial mortgage insurance premiums (IMIP) based on principal limit usage (PLU).

Initial Disbursement Limits

When homeowners take all of their available funds upfront, it increases the risk to FHA's Mutual Mortgage Insurance Fund (MMIF). This is the pool of money that insures FHA-insured loans and provides the non-recourse feature for HECM clients and their heirs. To address the increased risk, FHA changed the program to allow borrowers to only take large portions of their principal limits (>60%) during the first year when it is necessary to pay off large mortgages or mandatory obligations.

IMIP based on principal limit usage

Initial Mortgage Insurance Premiums are now based on how much the client needs to draw. Those borrowers who need no more than 60% of their principal limit at closing (fixed), or during the first year (ARM), will only pay 0.5% of their maximum claim amount in IMIP. Those borrowers who must exceed the 60% threshold will pay the higher premium of 2.5% of their maximum claim amount.

Let's look at REFERENCES

Mortgagee Letter 2013-27. INITIAL DISBURSEMENT LIMITS Term, Tenure, Line of Credit, Modified Term, and Modified Tenure Payment Options:
The maximum disbursement allowed at loan closing and during the First 12-Month Disbursement Period is the greater of sixty percent (60%) of the Principal Limit or the sum of Mandatory Obligations plus ten percent of the Principal Limit.

New Single Disbursement Lump Sum Payment Option:
The maximum disbursement allowed at loan closing is the greater of sixty percent (60%) of the Principal Limit or the sum of Mandatory Obligations plus ten percent of the Principal Limit.

2014 CHANGES

Non-Borrowing Spouses

The U.S. Department of Housing and Urban Development issued a mortgagee letter on April 25, 2014, outlining changes designed to protect non-borrowing spouses (NBS). According to Mortgagee Letter 2014-07, this changed "HECM program regulations and requirements concerning due and payable status where there is a non-borrowing spouse at the time of loan closing."

Upon the death of the last surviving borrower, non-borrowing spouses may be ELIGIBLE to remain in their homes. Keep in mind, a maturity event HAS indeed occurred, but "Due and

Payable" is simply DEFERRED to a later date. The mortgage will still accrue interest and mortgage insurance premiums. Also, no funds can be disbursed during the deferral period, except for funds set aside for designated repairs.

Let's look at REFERENCES
Mortgagee Letter 2014-07. NON-BORROWING SPOUSE
"Deferral Period" is defined as the period of time following the death of the last surviving mortgagor during which the due and payable status of a HECM is further deferred based on the continued satisfaction of the requirements for a Non-Borrowing Spouse under this ML and all other FHA requirements.

Seasoning Requirements
In the midst of so many other regulatory changes, many did not notice this December 2014 change. There are seasoning requirements now that prohibit homeowners from paying off existing liens unless they have been in place for more than 12 months or resulted in less than $500 cash to the homeowner.

The purpose of the seasoning requirement is to ensure that borrowers are not obtaining "gap financing" or interim financing to obtain Reverse Mortgages.

Let's look at REFERENCES
Mortgagee Letter 2014-21. Seasoning Requirements
Seasoning Requirements for Existing Non-HECM Liens Mortgagees may only permit the payoff of existing non-HECM liens using HECM proceeds if the liens have been in place longer for 12 months or resulted in less than $500 cash to the mortgagor, whether at closing or through cumulative draws (e.g., as with a Home Equity Line of Credit (HELOC)) prior to the date of the initial HECM loan application.

2015 Changes

Financial Assessment

Another major change became effective April 27, 2015 called Financial Assessment. For the first time, Reverse Mortgage lenders are required to assess each borrower's credit history, property charge history, and monthly residual income. Of course this was a dramatic change for an industry that historically focused on the value of the home.

When an underwriter determines that one or more of the financial assessment tests have failed, a Life Expectancy Set-Aside (or LESA) will be required. These are funds that are removed from the borrower's principal limit, and are set-aside for the purpose of paying property charges over a calculated time period.

Let's look at REFERENCES

HECM FINANCIAL ASSESSMENT AND PROPERTY CHARGE GUIDE

2.1 Credit History Analysis

The mortgagee must determine if the mortgagor has demonstrated the willingness to timely meet his or her financial obligations by analyzing the mortgagor's credit and property charge payment history.

3.1 Residual Income Analysis

The purpose of the cash flow/residual income analysis is to determine the capacity of the mortgagor to meet his or her documented financial obligations with his or her documented income.

Chapter 32

What are some HELPFUL HINTS
and RED FLAGS?

1. THE THREE-DAY RIGHT OF RESCISSION

"Closing" and "Funding" are not the same thing. So, don't panic when funds are not in the account right away. Most HECMs are refinances, and therefore have a three day "Right of Rescission." This means that within three days of closing, a homeowner can opt-out of the transaction. Funds cannot be wired until the fourth day. In addition, because of bank wiring times, borrowers should expect to see the funds in their account on the fifth day from closing.

2. LOWER INTEREST RATES ARE NOT ALWAYS BEST

There are circumstances under which a borrower might be helped by obtaining a higher rate on a fixed rate HECM, or even a higher lender margin and expected rate on the adjustable rate HECM. It actually happens quite frequently. The following are three reasons why this is true:

A. Lender Credits

The lender or broker will frequently offer credits toward closing costs for higher rates. If the objective is to keep the loan balance as low as possible in the short-run, it might be advantageous to accept a higher rate and reduce the closing costs. The trade-off is that higher rates will also increase the compounding of any loan balance the borrower might have.

B. Higher Tenure Payments

The expected interest rate (ER) is used to calculate the borrower's principal limits for the adjustable rate HECM products. However, the ER is ALSO used to calculate the TENURE PAYMENTS. Higher ERs may give the homeowner lower principal limits, but they may also convert to higher monthly payments.

Some say that if the borrower chooses the line of credit (LOC), then this advantage does not exist. That is not true. Many years later, if the borrower wants to convert his/her LOC to a tenure payment, the servicing department will annuitize the now higher net principal limit by using the ONLY expected rate in the system…the one we established at closing.

C. Higher Line of Credit (LOC) Growth

Remember, the available LOC can grow at the Interest Rate plus 1.25%. The lender margin is part of the interest rate calculation. Sure, higher lender margins will increase the compounding of the outstanding loan balance. But, if a borrower is carrying a low loan balance of $100, an extra 1% is only costing them an additional $1 per year. Meanwhile, the LOC of $200,000 grew by an extra $2,000 during that same time period.

3. WHEN IS YOUR NEXT BIRTHDAY?

The timing of the closing can impact how much the homeowner can receive. FHA uses whole ages to determine principal limits, and they round up. Therefore, if the youngest participant is within six months of his/her next birthday, FHA rounds up to the nearest age. The advantage is that the homeowner may qualify for more funds. If the homeowner is short to close by a little bit, then timing the closing might provide the additional needed funds.

4. WATCH OUT FOR THE 60% THRESHOLD

Be careful if the homeowner's mandatory obligations are between 50% and 60% of their principal limit. FHA allows the homeowner to take an additional 10% (of principal limit) ABOVE mandatory obligations. However, if this puts the homeowner above the 60% threshold, this would cost him/her an additional 2% in IMIP. Remember, LOW Principal Limit Usage (≤60%) brings an IMIP charge of 0.5%. Exceeding 60% brings an IMIP charge of 2.5%.

5. YOUR BROKER/LENDER CANNOT CROSS-SELL

Reverse Mortgage Professionals cannot require clients to buy annuities or any other financial instruments as a condition for getting a HECM. If this does occur, you may file a complaint with the CFPB at 1-855-411-CFPB (2372).

What do the REGULATIONS say?

Section 255 of the National Housing Act (12 U.S.C. 1715z–20). PROHIBITION AGAINST REQUIREMENTS TO PURCHASE ADDITIONAL PRODUCTS

The mortgagor or any other party shall not be required by the mortgagee or any other party to purchase an insurance, annuity, or other similar product as a requirement or condition of eligibility for insurance under subsection (c), except for title insurance, hazard, flood, or other peril insurance, or other such products that are customary and normal under subsection (c), as determined by the Secretary.

Chapter 33

What Should I Expect
During SERVICING?

When a HECM loan closes, the firm that originated the loan may, or may not, be the firm that services the loan. After all, there are only a handful of financial institutions that service these types of loans. Nevertheless, each loan is generally serviced in the same way according to HUD guidelines.

During servicing, the most critical borrower responsibilities are paying property charges and maintaining the property. However, there are other responsibilities and key concepts of which one should be aware. The following are the most common questions I receive related to servicing:

1. WHY DID I GET AN OCCUPANCY CERTIFICATION?

Reverse Mortgages are ONLY offered for primary residences. Therefore, the homeowner will be required to certify their occupancy of the property (via mail) exactly one year after closing and every year thereafter.

This is not an inspection of the property, and the homeowner should not feel that this is a violation of their privacy. The home-owner simply returns the signed certification indicating they still meet the requirements of the program. If the letter is not returned, the servicer may be required to follow up with phone calls and a visit to the property.

2. WILL I GET A MONTHLY STATEMENT?

Yes. Homeowners will get an activity statement so that they can keep track of their loan balances and their available lines-of-credit. According to Celink CEO, Jason McNamara,

"One of the basic functions of a Reverse Mortgage servicer is providing a monthly statement for each borrower that provides very useful information. It sounds like simple advice, but borrowers can greatly benefit and understand how their Reverse Mortgage is performing by reviewing their statements and loan balances every month. Borrowers who have used a Reverse Mortgage for a home equity line of credit can also keep track of those balances. Some borrowers don't know that their available lines of credit have increased, which can be a pleasant surprise."

3. HOW ARE PREPAYMENTS APPLIED?

One of the primary financial planning strategies is making periodic prepayments toward a HECM ARM loan balance. The result should be a reduction in the loan balance, and a corresponding increase to the borrower's available line-of-credit.

When payments are made to reduce a HECM loan balance, however, those payments are applied to different accounting buckets in a progression known as the servicing waterfall shown here:

1st – Initial Mortgage Insurance (IMIP),

2nd – Accrued Mortgage Insurance (MIP),

3rd – Servicing fees (if charged),

4th – Interest accruals, and then

5th – Principal

This means that homeowners will have to pay back ALL of their accrued mortgage insurance before they will be eligible for mortgage interest deductions.

However, the servicing waterfall is only important for tax and accounting purposes, and it should not impact the borrower's ability to draw those prepaid funds again on a HECM ARM. Any reduction in loan balance should increase the available LOC.

4. WHY DID I GET AN IRS FORM 1098?

Does this mean the homeowners owe taxes? No. But this does create some confusion for Reverse Mortgage borrowers every January, because loan servicers are required to notify each borrower when any prepayments exceed $600.

Most Reverse Mortgage borrowers won't get a 1098, simply because most of them don't make prepayments toward their loan balances. Some will, however, as we have just described the advantages.

Reverse Mortgage professionals are generally not tax professionals. Yet, their borrowers need to know that the IRS Form 1098 lists items that were paid BY the borrower. This is for tax and accounting purposes, and does not INCREASE tax liability. In fact, the Form 1098 is used to report potential deductions, and therefore may REDUCE tax liability. For our purposes though, it means that the borrowers made prepayments during the previous year that were applied to either their accrued mortgage insurance and/or their accrued mortgage interest.

The IRS deduction for Mortgage **INSURANCE** (itemized in Box 5 for tax year 2016) has been renewed by congress in recent years. However, this deduction is very limited, and borrowers may not be able to write-off that amount. Borrowers are advised to consult their tax planners.

The IRS deduction for Mortgage **INTEREST** (itemized in Box 1 for tax year 2016), however, is more likely to be deducted. Of course it will depend on other factors that borrowers should, once again, discuss with their tax professionals.

5. WHY IS HUD SERVICING MY LOAN?

HECM loans can be assigned to The U.S. Department of Housing and Urban Development (HUD) for many reasons. The most common reason is the loan balance is approaching the Maximum Claim Amount (MCA). Remember, the MCA is the lesser of the home's value at origination or the HECM loan limit (currently $636,150). Lenders/Servicers can submit a loan to HUD when a loan balance reaches 97.5% of MCA, but it cannot be approved until a loan reaches 98%.

Documents were also signed at closing which allow HUD to service the loan when the lender is unable to distribute the required funds to the borrower. While lenders/servicers are unlikely to go out of business while maintaining a servicing portfolio, it is nice to know that HUD will make sure home-owners always have access to their funds.

Let's look at REFERENCES

HUD Handbook 4235.1 Chapter 5-12C: Partial Prepayment.
A borrower may choose to make a partial prepayment to set up or to increase a line of credit without altering existing monthly payments. By reducing the outstanding balance, the borrower increases the net principal limit. All or part of the increase in the net principal limit may be set aside for a line of credit.

24 C.F.R. § 206.107: Mortgagee election of assignment.
Under the assignment option, the mortgagee shall have the option of assigning the mortgage to the Secretary if the mortgage balance is equal to or greater than 98 percent of the maximum claim amount, or the mortgagor has requested a payment which exceeds the difference between the maximum claim amount and the mortgage balance...

HUD 4330.1 Appendix 68—2.7.4. Partial Prepayments.
A Borrower receiving monthly payments in combination with a line of credit may specify to which account a partial prepayment is to be applied. If Borrower does not designate an account, Lender shall apply any partial prepayments to an existing line of credit or create a new line of credit.

Chapter 34

What is a
HECM-to-HECM REFINANCE?

With a HECM to HECM refinance (also known as a H2H Refi), the borrower will be paying off an existing HECM with a new HECM.

These Reverse Mortgages are a little different from traditional HECMs that pay off existing forward liens. In fact, the National Reverse Mortgage Lenders Association (NRMLA) recently issued updated guidelines to prevent "loan flipping" or "churning", a practice where a loan originator repeatedly refinances an existing HECM borrower with no bona fide advantage to the borrower.

WHY WOULD SOMEONE
REFINANCE THEIR HECM ANYWAY?

The HECMs with Adjustable Rate Mortgages (HECM ARMs) have a built-in disincentive to refinance—the borrower's net principal limit (how much they can borrow) continues to grow over time. This means that homeowners who have not borrowed all of their available funds have a growing line-of-credit that often makes refinancing unnecessary.

However, there are many legitimate reasons why a current Reverse Mortgage client may want to refinance into a new one.

Reasons why seniors may want to refinance their HECMs:

- A homeowner who is recently married may want his/her new spouse added to title and be listed on the note. With a H2H Refi, the new spouse would have additional protection that the Reverse Mortgage offers.

- Property values may have increased, offering the homeowner additional funds.

- A H2H Refi may be needed if the homeowner wishes to change loan programs (Fixed Rate or ARM), or if they wish to reduce their interest rate.

One additional reason for a H2H Refi is that prior to 2008, many homes were capped by FHA county lending limits that reduced the amount of funds available for higher-priced homes. In 2008, the Housing and Economic Recovery Act (HERA) established a higher national lending limit ($417,000), and then it raised again in 2009 ($625,500). For this reason, homeowners with higher-valued homes who obtained their HECMs more than 6 years ago, might find the program even more attractive today.

WHAT IS THE IMIP CREDIT?

One nice advantage is that the borrower should get a CREDIT for the amount of Initial Mortgage Insurance Premium (IMIP) they paid on their last transaction. This happens regardless of how long it has been since their previous closing.

The following example shows IMIP from a standard HECM applied to a NEW HECM:

	Original HECM	New HECM
Max Claim Amount	$100,000	$120,000
IMIP	$2,000 (2%)	$3,000 (2.5%)
		− $2,000
Adjusted IMIP After Credit		= $1,000

WHAT ARE THE UPDATED GUIDELINES?

The following are recent NRMLA guidelines/restrictions that are designed to prevent "loan flipping" or "churning" of Reverse Mortgages:

1. **The 18 Month SEASONING REQUIREMENT is easy...the new FHA case number shall be no sooner than 18 months from the date of the prior closing.**

Even after 18 months, there must be a "bona fide advantage" to the consumer. This means that the refinance will need to originate from a written request to add a family member to the loan, OR the following 2 tests must be passed:

2. **The CLOSING COST TEST is a little more complex. The increase in principal limit must be at least 5X the costs of the transaction.**

For example, a loan with $5,000 in closing costs must produce an increase in principal limit of at least $25,000.

3. **THE LOAN PROCEEDS TEST is the newest guideline. The available benefit amount from the refinance must be at least 5% of the borrower's principal limit.**

For example, a borrower with a $200,000 NEW Principal Limit must have at least $10,000 in funds generated by the refinance. These available funds, also known as "Net Principal Limit", may be drawn at closing, held in a Line-of-Credit, or distributed over time in the form of monthly payments.

HOW DO I PROCEED WITH A H2H REFI?

The borrower will need to obtain a "HECM Servicer Refi Worksheet." This document from their current servicer will show their original Maximum Claim Amount (MCA), how much they paid in Initial Mortgage Insurance (IMIP), and the date of their last transaction. Keep in mind, prior to 2009 there were county lending limits in place. Therefore, their appraisal may have been much higher than their MCA.

Let's look at REFERENCES ——————————
NRMLA Ethics Advisory Opinion 2015-2
In addition to the requirement that the HECM Refinance have a case number assignment date that is at least eighteen (18) months after the closing date of the prior HECM loan being refinanced, for a HECM Refinance to provide the required bona fide advantage to a consumer, the HECM Refinance shall either:

(a) Be originated at the written request of the current HECM loan mortgagor to add as a mortgagor under the HECM Refinance a non-borrowing spouse or other member of the current mortgagor's family, who is residing in the principal residence of the current mortgagor and who is otherwise qualified to be a mortgagor; or

(b) Pass both a Closing Cost Test and a Loan Proceeds Test as each of those terms is further defined, below, in this Ethics Advisory Opinion 2015-2.

Mortgagee Letter 2013-27
For all refinance transactions, mortgagees and counselors must use the formula below to determine the amount of initial MIP due to HUD.

(1) New MCA multiplied by *new initial MIP (%) = New MIP
(2) Old MCA multiplied by old initial MIP (%) = Old MIP
(3) Subtracting the result of (2) from the result of (1) yields the MIP amount owed to HUD

Chapter 35

What are the NEXT STEPS?

Leveraging your hard-earned home equity can be a difficult choice. The HECM program may be challenging to understand. I wrote this book with the expressed purpose to help people better UNDERSTAND REVERSE.

For you, your heirs, or your Reverse Mortgage Professional (RMP), this is not something to take lightly. In addition, you should NEVER feel pressured into a decision. **The best RMPs are educators, not salespeople.** Take your time, develop a relationship with an experienced HECM professional, and make the right choice for you and your family.

You have taken the first step by choosing to educate yourself by reading this book.

HERE IS A 10-STEP PROCESS FOR A HOMEOWNER TO MOVE FORWARD:

1. **Initial Discussion:** Review the HECM product with a Reverse Mortgage Professional (RMP) that is licensed in your area. Again, some forward mortgage professionals are not aware of the intricacies involved in originating HECMs.

2. **Pre-Counseling Package:** Obtain this from the RMP. It should include the following documentation:

   - Counseling list that includes numbers for national and local agencies

   - "Preparing for Your Counseling Session" document

   - Loan Comparison of various product options

   - Total Annual Loan Cost (TALC) rate disclosure

   - Amortization Schedule

   - "Use Your Home to Stay at Home" booklet from NCOA

3. **Counseling:** Complete a counseling session with a HUD-approved counselor, with all required parties involved. The counselor will send certificates which must be signed and dated by all parties. The lender is restricted in what they can do until a fully signed and dated counseling certificate is provided.

4. **Loan Application:** Contact your RMP to complete the application, which is called a "Form 1009." Additional disclosures will need to be signed at that time.

5. **Appraisal:** An appraiser will visit your home to take pictures and measurements. They will generate a report of comparable sales which will be used by the underwriter to determine the current value of the home.

6. **Processing:** A processor will likely contact you to collect additional information necessary to send the loan file to an underwriter.

7. **Underwriting:** The underwriter is the final decision-maker regarding critical elements of the loan, and makes sure that the loan file is in order.

8. **Closing:** When the loan is approved by the underwriter, the loan may be cleared to close, and closing may be scheduled.

9. **Servicing:** When closed, your loan will be handled by one of only a handful of loan servicers that specialize in HECM loans.

10. **Please recommend this book to your friends, family, and neighbors.**

KEY TERMS

ADJUSTABLE RATE HECM (HECM ARM): These are variable rate loans. The rate will change monthly or annually, and are tied to the movements of the London Interbank Offered Rate (LIBOR) index.

CAP: This limits the amount that an adjustable interest rate may go up or down during a specified time period. The capped rate will be listed in the note.

CERTIFIED REVERSE MORTGAGE PROFESSIONAL (CRMP): This designation, administered by the National Reverse Mortgage Lenders Association, requires testing and regular continuing education requirements.

EXPECTED RATE (ER): The expected rate is used to determine the principal limit on a HECM loan, not current interest rates. On a Fixed Rate HECM, the expected rate is the same as the interest rate, and it does not change over time. With the HECM ARM, the expected rate equals the 10-year SWAP rate plus the lenders margin.

FEDERAL HOUSING ADMINISTRATION (FHA): An agency within the U.S. Department of Housing and Urban Development (HUD) that issues insurance to private lenders for forward as well as reverse (HECM) loans.

FIXED RATE HECM: The rates for this product will never change over the life of the loan and the product is often referred to as HECM-Fixed.

HECM (Home Equity Conversion Mortgage): Commonly referred to as a Reverse Mortgage. The program is designed to enable homeowners, age 62 and over, to convert a portion of the equity in their homes to cash, monthly streams of income, and/or lines-of-credit. The FHA insures the HECM if all program guidelines are met.

HECM for PURCHASE (H4P): This is a unique home loan program for home buyers 62 and older. It allows them to purchase a primary residence with no required monthly principal or interest mortgage payments. Title to the property is transferred to the new mortgagor, who will then occupy the property as a primary residence within 60 days of the closing.

HECM to HECM REFI (H2H): This is a Reverse Mortgage variation that allows a current HECM borrower to refinance into a new HECM loan after a minimum of 18 months. The borrower will generally receive a full credit of any up-front mortgage insurance applied to the new up-front MIP.

HUD (The U.S. Department of Housing and Urban Development): A federal agency that oversees the Federal Housing Administration and numerous housing and community development programs.

INITIAL DISBURSEMENT LIMIT: At closing (FIXED) or during the first year (ARM), HECM borrowers are restricted in their disbursements. The limit will be the greater of 60% of the principal limit, or the mandatory obligations plus 10% of the principal limit.

INITIAL MORTGAGE INSURANCE PREMIUM (IMIP): Also called up-front MIP, this will be 0.5% or 2.5%, depending on the borrower's principal limit utilization. This is paid to the federal government for insuring the loan.

LIBOR (LIBOR Index): The London Interbank Offered Rate is the index that is added to the lender margin to arrive at a current interest rate. For HECM transactions, we are specifically talking about the 1-month LIBOR Index or the 1-year LIBOR Index.

LINE OF CREDIT (LOC): When the borrower does not access all of his/her principal limit, the remainder may be available in a credit line. This popular payout option is available for adjustable rate HECM products, and allows a portion of the borrower's principal limit to be available for future use. Funds that are available in a LOC will grow, will be secure, and will be available for future use, but will not accrue interest or mortgage insurance charges.

MANDATORY OBLIGATIONS: These are items that must be paid off at closing, including: mortgages, liens, judgments that affect their home's title, federal debt, closing costs, and initial mortgage insurance premiums, etc. These may be financed into the loan, or paid by the homeowner at closing.

MARGIN (Lender Margin): For adjustable rate HECMs, this is the percentage added to the LIBOR index. This is for the lender's benefit, and the combination of the two numbers will equal the current interest rate. For example, if the lender margin is 3%, and the LIBOR Index is 1%, the resulting interest rate would be 4%. The margin portion of the interest rate never changes over the life of the loan.

MAXIMUM CLAIM AMOUNT (MCA): This is generally the lesser of the home's value or the HECM lending limit, which is a nationwide loan limit of $636,150. We can still originate loans on homes valued over this threshold, but a homeowner's available funds will be calculated as if the home was valued at $636,150.

MODIFIED TENURE: A combination of tenure payments and a line of credit.

MODIFIED TERM: A combination of term payments and a line of credit.

MORTGAGE INSURANCE PREMIUM (MIP): Insurance premiums are collected in two forms: Initial MIP (IMIP) that is paid as a closing cost, and Annual MIP that is added to the loan balance. Most clients will finance both as part of their HECM loan balance.

MORTGAGEE: This is another word for the MORTGAGE LENDER. I refer to this as "the lender," but the HECM guidelines and federal regulations may use the term "mortgagee."

MORTGAGOR: This is another word for the BORROWER in a mortgage transaction. I refer to this as "the borrower," but the HECM guidelines and federal regulations may use the term "mortgagor."

NATIONAL REVERSE MORTGAGE LENDER'S ASSOCIATION (NRMLA): This is the national voice of the Reverse Mortgage industry, serving as an educational resource, policy advocate, and public affairs center for lenders and related professionals.

NON-BORROWING SPOUSE (NBS): This is the spouse of a HECM borrower who is NOT a party to the loan. One of the reasons for this designation is that only those age 62 and older can obtain a HECM. However, HUD has determined that for loans with FHA case numbers issued on Aug. 4, 2014 and later, a spouse of a HECM borrower will have additional rights. Despite not being on title, a non-borrowing spouse may continue to stay in the home as long as certain requirements are met.

NON-RECOURSE FEATURE: With a HECM, the homeowner and his/her heirs will not owe more than the home is worth at the time it is sold. There is no recourse to the borrower for a deficiency at the time of sale. This is a tremendous feature of the HECM program since it removes much of the risk associated with homeownership.

ORIGINATION FEE: This is a one-time fee paid to the lender at the time the loan closes. With a HECM, the maximum origination fee is 2% on the initial $200,000 in home value, and 1% on the value thereafter with a cap of $6,000. FHA does allow a minimum of $2,500 regardless of value.

PRIMARY RESIDENCE: This is the property a homeowner occupies for 183 days or more annually (> 50% of the year). A Reverse Mortgage can only be obtained on a primary residence, or one that will be the primary residence in 60 days.

PRINCIPAL LIMIT FACTORS (PLF): These are percentages, and are similar to what the forward mortgage industry refers to as Loan-to-Value (LTV). In our industry, however, we use PLF tables to determine how much a lender can offer a homeowner. These tables, published by HUD, tell us the percentage of a borrower's home value for which he/she initially qualifies. PLFs will vary, based on the age of the youngest participant and the expected interest rate (ER) of the loan.

PRINCIPAL LIMIT (PL): This is expressed in dollars, and represents the client's maximum borrowing capacity. Initially it is calculated by multiplying the borrower's maximum claim amount by the principal limit factor (PLF). From this principal limit, the lender will pay off mortgages or liens that affect title, delinquent federal debt, and any costs associated with the loan. The remainder is call the Net Principal Limit (NPL).

PRINCIPAL RESIDENCE: This is where the homeowner maintains his/her abode for the majority of the year: 183 days or more. A borrower can only have one principal, or primary, residence at a time.

REVERSE MORTGAGE: A financial tool which provides homeowners with funds from the equity in their homes. Generally, no payments are made on Reverse Mortgages until the borrower moves or the property is sold.

TENURE PAYMENT: Tenure means permanent, and is a payout option on HECM ARM products. It allows the borrower(s) to receive equal monthly payments for as long as any borrower is able to occupy the home and abide by program guidelines. The borrowers will continue to receive funds on this program regardless of how long they live, even if their home values decline.

TERM PAYMENT: Term means for a period of time. On the adjustable rate products, this payout option allows the borrower(s) to receive equal monthly payments for a fixed number of months. Longer terms will offer the borrower smaller payments, while shorter terms will offer the borrower larger payments.

QUICK REFERENCE GUIDE

HECM Principal Limit Factor (PLF) Tables are published by HUD and change periodically. The most recent change was 8/4/2014, and these PLFs are still in effect when this edition of the Understanding Reverse was completed. Please note this PLF table is subject to change at any time.

PLFs are based on both the <u>relevant age</u> and the <u>expected rate</u> of the HECM loan.

Note: • Any expected rate that rounds to 5.00% or less, will receive the maximum PLF for that age.

• Any age at, or above, age 90 will receive the maximum PLF for that expected rate.

The **relevant age** is the nearest age of the of the youngest borrower (or eligible non-borrowing spouse) at the time of closing. Therefore, if the closing date is set within six months of the next birthday, the age will be rounded up, and borrower will generally qualify for more funds.

The **expected rate** is also rounded, and it will round to the nearest 1/8% when calculating PLFs. For example, 5.06% rounds down to 5% when referencing the table. Unfortunately, 5.07% would round up to 5.125%, and the borrower would generally qualify for less funds.

By knowing the relevant age and rate, you can use this handy reference sheet to quickly see the maximum percentage of a home's value a lender may currently offer a borrower.

While the full PLF tables begin at 3% and change every .125% up to 18.875%, this Quick Reference Guide only displays commonly used expected rates between 5.0% and 6.0% for the HECM products.

CHART 1

This section of the PLF table is for borrowers and spouses who are already 62 or older.

Age	5.000%	5.125%	5.250%	5.375%	5.500%	5.625%	5.750%	5.875%	6.000%
62	52.4%	50.8%	49.1%	47.5%	45.9%	44.3%	42.7%	41.1%	39.5%
63	53.0%	51.4%	49.8%	48.2%	46.6%	44.9%	43.3%	41.7%	40.1%
64	53.6%	52.0%	50.4%	48.8%	47.2%	45.6%	44.0%	42.3%	40.7%
65	54.2%	52.6%	51.0%	49.4%	47.8%	46.2%	44.6%	43.0%	41.4%
66	54.9%	53.3%	51.7%	50.1%	48.5%	46.9%	45.3%	43.7%	42.1%
67	55.6%	54.0%	52.4%	50.8%	49.2%	47.6%	46.0%	44.4%	42.9%
68	56.2%	54.7%	53.1%	51.5%	49.9%	48.3%	46.8%	45.2%	43.6%
69	56.9%	55.3%	53.8%	52.2%	50.6%	49.1%	47.5%	45.9%	44.3%
70	57.6%	56.0%	54.4%	52.9%	51.3%	49.8%	48.2%	46.7%	45.1%
71	58.3%	56.8%	55.2%	53.7%	52.1%	50.6%	49.0%	47.5%	45.9%
72	59.1%	57.5%	56.0%	54.5%	52.9%	51.4%	49.8%	48.3%	46.7%
73	59.9%	58.3%	56.8%	55.2%	53.7%	52.2%	50.6%	49.1%	47.5%
74	60.6%	59.1%	57.5%	56.0%	54.5%	53.0%	51.4%	49.9%	48.4%
75	61.4%	59.8%	58.3%	56.8%	55.3%	53.7%	52.2%	50.7%	49.2%
76	62.2%	60.7%	59.2%	57.7%	56.2%	54.7%	53.1%	51.6%	50.1%
77	63.1%	61.6%	60.1%	58.6%	57.1%	55.6%	54.1%	52.6%	51.0%
78	64.0%	62.5%	61.0%	59.5%	58.0%	56.5%	55.0%	53.5%	52.0%
79	64.8%	63.3%	61.8%	60.4%	58.9%	57.4%	55.9%	54.4%	52.9%
80	65.7%	64.2%	62.7%	61.2%	59.8%	58.3%	56.8%	55.3%	53.9%
81	66.5%	65.1%	63.6%	62.1%	60.7%	59.2%	57.8%	56.3%	54.9%
82	67.4%	65.9%	64.5%	63.1%	61.6%	60.2%	58.8%	57.3%	55.9%
83	68.2%	66.8%	65.4%	64.0%	62.5%	61.1%	59.7%	58.3%	56.9%
84	69.0%	67.6%	66.3%	64.9%	63.5%	62.1%	60.7%	59.3%	57.9%
85	69.9%	68.5%	67.1%	65.8%	64.4%	63.0%	61.7%	60.3%	58.9%
86	70.9%	69.5%	68.2%	66.8%	65.5%	64.1%	62.8%	61.5%	60.1%
87	71.9%	70.6%	69.2%	67.9%	66.6%	65.3%	63.9%	62.6%	61.3%
88	72.9%	71.6%	70.3%	69.0%	67.7%	66.4%	65.1%	63.8%	62.5%
89	73.9%	72.6%	71.4%	70.1%	68.8%	67.5%	66.2%	64.9%	63.6%
90	75.0%	73.7%	72.4%	71.1%	69.9%	68.6%	67.3%	66.1%	64.8%

CHART 2

Because eligible Non-Borrowing Spouses (NBS) may be under age 62, supplemental PLFs were added to the tables in 2014.

Age	5.000%	5.125%	5.250%	5.375%	5.500%	5.625%	5.750%	5.875%	6.000%
18-19	31.7%	30.6%	29.5%	28.5%	27.4%	26.3%	25.2%	24.2%	23.1%
20-24	32.6%	31.5%	30.4%	29.3%	28.2%	27.1%	26.0%	24.9%	23.8%
25-29	35.0%	33.8%	32.6%	31.4%	30.2%	29.0%	27.8%	26.6%	25.4%
30-34	37.3%	36.0%	34.7%	33.4%	32.2%	30.9%	29.6%	28.3%	27.0%
35-39	39.6%	38.3%	36.9%	35.5%	34.1%	32.8%	31.4%	30.0%	28.7%
40-44	42.0%	40.5%	39.1%	37.6%	36.1%	34.7%	33.2%	31.8%	30.3%
45-49	44.3%	42.8%	41.2%	39.7%	38.1%	36.6%	35.0%	33.5%	31.9%
50-54	46.0%	44.5%	43.0%	41.5%	40.0%	38.4%	36.9%	35.4%	33.9%
55	48.4%	46.8%	45.2%	43.6%	41.9%	40.3%	38.7%	37.1%	35.5%
56	48.9%	47.3%	45.7%	44.1%	42.5%	40.9%	39.3%	37.7%	36.0%
57	49.5%	47.9%	46.3%	44.6%	43.0%	41.4%	39.8%	38.2%	36.6%
58	50.0%	48.4%	46.8%	45.2%	43.6%	42.0%	40.4%	38.7%	37.1%
59	50.6%	49.0%	47.4%	45.7%	44.1%	42.5%	40.9%	39.3%	37.7%
60	51.1%	49.5%	47.9%	46.3%	44.7%	43.1%	41.5%	39.8%	38.2%
61	51.7%	50.1%	48.5%	46.9%	45.3%	43.7%	42.1%	40.5%	38.9%

Let's look at REFERENCES

Mortgagee Letter 2014-12. New Principal Limit Factors

The new Principal Limit Factor (PLF) tables have been wholly revised and now also include PLFs for use where the Borrower has a Non-Borrowing Spouse younger than 62.

Notes: _____
_____
_____
_____
_____
_____
_____
_____
_____
_____
_____
_____
_____
_____
_____
_____
_____
_____
_____
_____